Village
in
LANCASHIRE

Nick Burton

COUNTRYSIDE BOOKS
NEWBURY, BERKSHIRE

First published 1998
© Nick Burton 1998

COUNTRYSIDE BOOKS
3 Catherine Road
Newbury, Berkshire

ISBN 1 85306 501 3

To my Mum

Designed by Graham Whiteman
Illustrations by Trevor Yorke
Maps and photographs by the author

Produced through MRM Associates Ltd., Reading
Printed by J. W. Arrowsmith Ltd., Bristol

Contents

Area Map Showing Locations of the Walks.

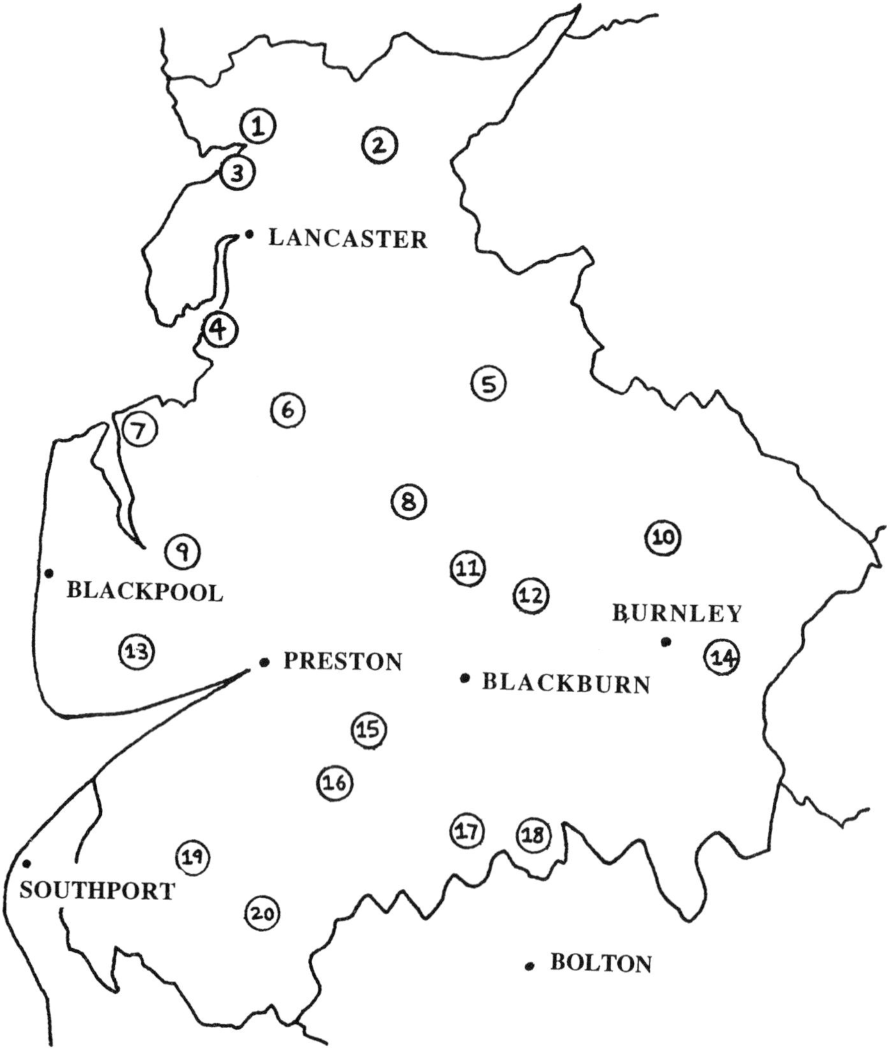

① ②

③

• LANCASTER

④

⑤

⑥

⑦

⑧

⑩

⑨ ⑪ ⑫

• BLACKPOOL BURNLEY

⑬ ⑭

• PRESTON • BLACKBURN

⑮

⑯

⑰ ⑱

⑲

SOUTHPORT ⑳

• BOLTON

WALK

Publisher's Note

We hope that you obtain considerable enjoyment from this book; great care has been taken in its preparation. Although at the time of publication all routes followed public rights of way or permitted paths, diversion orders can be made and permissions withdrawn.

We cannot of course be held responsible for such diversion orders and any inaccuracies in the text which result from these or any other changes to the routes nor any damage which might result from walkers trespassing on private property. We are anxious though that all details covering the walks are kept up to date and would therefore welcome information from readers which would be relevant to future editions.

Introduction

Written histories of the county of Lancashire have, more often than not, concentrated on the great achievements of its textile towns rather than the long history of its villages. But the county did not begin with 18th century cotton mills and coal mines, so through this series of walks I hope that at least a handful of Lancashire villages can step back into the limelight. In fact, Lancashire's village heritage is no poorer than many other shire counties. The Romans settled here, as did the succeeding waves of wild Dark Age invaders – the Angles, Saxons, Danes and Norsemen – whose significant legacy has been the village names themselves. They also established places of worship and many succeeding medieval churches were placed upon the same ancient holy sites. The Middle Ages saw the rise of great Lancashire abbeys and the emergence of noble families who built fine country mansions, many of which survive today. Indeed, Lancashire is well endowed with historic old homes and schools. Many of these homes came under attack in the English Civil War in the 17th century as the county was divided in its support for the King or Cromwell. In Tudor and Stuart times Lancashire villages enjoyed a heyday as flourishing market centres for rural produce. So, long before the Industrial Revolution there was life in Lancashire.

The county's industrial trades actually began in the villages – for example, domestic weaving, which was eventually succeeded in the 18th century by the abrupt appearance of a rural cotton mill in many villages. The moorland brooks of South and East Lancashire gave birth to many 'new' industrial villages. Transport developments like the turnpike roads, canals and the railways were a further impetus to village growth and during this era of great industrial change even the ancient Lancashire villages doubled their populations and physical size.

There is really no better way to discover the rich tapestry of history woven in Lancashire's villages than by exploring them on foot. The settlements existed long before cars and were not fashioned to accommodate such forms of transport. I accept that in the absence of an efficient public transport system – though Lancashire is better than many other counties in this department – the car is a necessary evil to reach even the starting point of country walks. However, the lifeblood of any village is its inhabitants, and Lancashire has an abundance of villagers who really care for their environment. Therefore, please use the utmost discretion when parking vehicles. Car parking locations are indicated in the text – but if they are full, or for some reason unusable, do ensure that you park your vehicle in such a way as not to be a nuisance to those who live close by.

The villages in this collection have been chosen intentionally to enable the walker to experience something of all the diverse landscapes and geographical areas in the county. The rough list of these (from north to south) is as follows: Silverdale limestone, the Lune valley, Morecambe Bay, the Forest of Bowland, the Wyre valley, the Fylde plain, the Ribble valley, the Pennines, the West Pennine Moors and the West Lancashire plain. At least one village, often several, has been picked from each of these areas so that the walker can gain an intimacy with the whole of Lancashire.

The suggested walks are all circular and are illustrated by sketch maps, designed to guide you to the starting point and provide a simple yet accurate idea of the route to be taken. However, for those who like the benefit of detailed maps, the various Ordnance Survey sheets are very much recommended, especially for identifying the main features of views. I have given the relevant numbers of the Landranger (1:50 000) series in each case.

Places where food and drink can be obtained are also given for each walk. Opening times have not been included due to the fact that they can often change. However, these can be obtained by using the relevant telephone numbers provided. The same goes for the list of attractions mentioned. Again, if you are planning a visit I would advise that you contact the place concerned to confirm it will be open.

The final words I leave to William Wilkie Collins who sums it up quite nicely: 'walk, and be merry; walk, and be healthy; walk, and be your own master!'

Nick Burton

WARTON
Length: 8½ miles

Getting there: The village is less than 1 mile from the A6 and M6, just 1½ miles north of Carnforth. If approaching from the M6 leave at junction 35. **Parking:** The walk starts below	Warton Crag. Ideally, park at the free car park in the old quarry on Crag Road – this lane runs alongside the Black Bull and the car park is signposted from the main village street. Alternatively, parking space	may be found along the main street. **Map:** OS Landranger 97 Kendal to Morecambe (GR 498724).

American tourists are no strangers to the winding lanes of this dour grey village and can be glimpsed clicking their expensive cameras in the direction of St Oswald's church, just down the hill from the Black Bull. They make a pilgrimage to Warton to capture a unique piece of American his-

tory. Rescued from the outside of St Oswald's 15th-century tower is a weathered stone flag – now kept indoors – inscribed with the coat of arms of the Washington family who lived in Warton from the Middle Ages until 1823. The first American president, George Washington, was a relative of the Warton clan and a pattern on the coat of arms is believed to have inspired the design of the 'stars and stripes' on the American flag.

Almost opposite St Oswald's are the remains of the Old Rectory, a 14th-century manor house which pre-dates the present church. Looming behind the village is the distinctive wooded limestone hill of Warton Crag which was an ancient defensive site to warn of possible invaders from Scotland. The Crag was occupied by an ancient hillfort as well as being one of a long chain of beacons warning of the approach of the Spanish Armada in the 16th century.

The greater mileage involved in this walk is worthwhile to explore in depth this magical lump of limestone country perched at the very top of the Lancashire coast. Starting from the quarry car park on Crag Road, the walk skirts Warton Crag Nature Reserve and follows an old bridle road to Jenny Brown's Point. The route then follows lanes and paths through Silverdale's limestone woodlands to arrive at Leighton Moss RSPB reserve and then continues to stately Leighton Hall, climbing uphill to enjoy views which are a fitting climax to the walk.

THE WALK

❶ From the quarry car park take the path which leads uphill through trees to reach a gate. Turn right along a track and follow it for ½ mile along the edge of the limestone woodland – keeping a boundary wall and fields close by to your right. Please note this is a permissive route kindly provided as one of a number of trails through Warton Crag Nature Reserve. Eventually, by an information board, a wall is reached with a gap in it. Go through the gap to join a stone road.

❷ Turn left along the road – an old bridleway – and follow it uphill between walls for about 1¼ miles. The track eventually drops down to join a lane at Crag Foot.

❸ Turn right along the lane which drops downhill to join another road. Turn right and follow the pavement as the road swings sharp left heading towards a railway. The prominent chimney to your right marks the site of a former pump house built to drain Leighton Moss prior to 1917. Look out for the first footpath sign on the left of the road which is signposted for Jenny Brown's Point.

❹ Leave the road here and follow the track under the railway. On the far side of the railway turn right and follow the Lancashire Coastal Way waymarkers which lead across a stream, through a gate and then veer left to cross a stile and follow the wide embankment between the marsh and fields. At the bottom of a hill turn left and follow the shore path which leads to a chimney – the remains of an 18th-century copper smelting mill. Continue in front of the picturesque cottages to join the end of a narrow lane.

❺ Continue straight ahead along the lane and when it swings right look out for a kissing gate in the wall to your left which leads into the National Trust property of Jack Scout. Go through the kissing gate and follow the grass path which runs parallel to the road. Acquired by the National Trust in 1982, Jack Scout is a lovely little promontory of great interest. The path leads to a renovated old lime kiln and then rejoins the lane through a kissing gate. Turn left and follow the lane to a road junction.

❻ Turn right at the junction and follow Hollins Lane which is signposted for Carnforth. The road leads past Wolf House Gallery and climbs slightly uphill, bending to the left. Look out for two footpath signposts on the left-hand side of the road after the bend and go through the squeeze stile and down the steps to join them.

❼ Take the path which forks right, signposted for Stankelt Road – this leads through woodland alongside a field then runs above a steep crag. The path emerges from the woodland at a stile which leads into a field. Swing right from the stile and climb the grass bank to an old signpost, then turn left and cross further stiles to follow a path through more woodland. A wall side is joined on the right and the

The renovated old lime kiln at Jack Scout, which is passed on the walk.

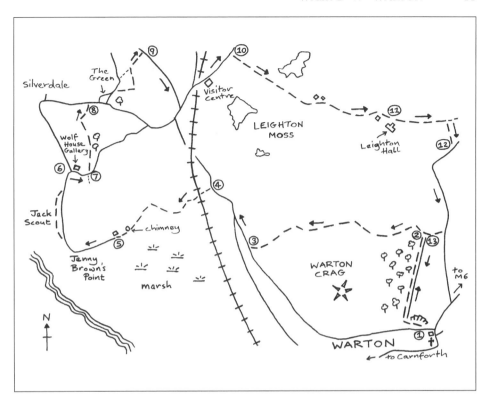

path leads to a wooden gate of a private property. Turn right here and follow the fenced path between the field and houses. Cross over a stone stile and turn right to join a road.

❽ Turn right and follow the road for just 80 yards before turning up the little alleyway signposted as The Green. Follow the alley which leads to another lane, Bottoms Lane. Turn left and take the public footpath on the right, signposted for Burton's Well and Lambert's Meadow. The track leads through woodland and enters Lambert's Meadow via a gate. Turn right over the little footbridge and follow the path to the opposite side of the meadow, which is

owned by the National Trust. Climb the steep steps through woodland to emerge at a lane alongside a cottage.

❾ Turn right and follow the lane downhill to a busier road. Turn left onto the main road and follow it towards Silverdale railway station. Before reaching the station turn right down the adjoining road which leads over the railway line to Leighton Moss Nature Reserve visitor centre. Continue along the road past the reserve for ¼ mile until a footpath sign for Yealand Conyers is reached on the right-hand side.

❿ Leave the road here and follow the

causeway which cuts a straight course through the high reed beds of Leighton Moss – the largest remaining tract of reed bed in the north-west of England. Beyond a gate, follow the track which winds past farm buildings until shortly the turrets of Leighton Hall come into view. Go straight ahead to reach the driveway entrance to the Hall. Built upon the ancient family seat of the Middletons, the present Hall dates from the 18th century with a 19th-century Gothic façade inspired by Sir Walter Scott.

⓫ Unless you are visiting the Hall, continue straight ahead and leave the driveway when it swings right. Veer slightly left up the steep hill slope, following the line of the telegraph poles. The reward for the steep climb is the exceptional views across Morecambe Bay. Turn right at the top of the hill and follow the path which runs along the top, passing through kissing gates to join a lane.

⓬ Turn right and follow the lane downhill. Keep to the lane for ¾ mile; it passes the main entrance to Leighton Hall and swings left, eventually running downhill to meet a bridleway on the right-hand side, signposted for Crag Road. Turn right up this stone road for about 120 yards before reaching the gap in the wall on your left.

⓭ Retrace your steps along the permissive route which skirts the edge of the woodland back to the quarry car park. On reaching the car park continue down Crag Road to explore the village.

ARKHOLME

Length: 3¾ miles

Getting there: The village is situated along the B6254, 6 miles east of Carnforth and 5 miles south of Kirkby Lonsdale. If approaching from	the M6, leave at junction 35. **Parking:** Along the main village street. Try and park at the end closest to the crossroads by the	Bay Horse as the walk starts from here. **Map:** OS Landranger 97 Kendal to Morecambe (GR 583722).

From the riverside bluff on which Arkholme's medieval parish church now stands, Norman invaders kept guard over the approaches of the river Lune. It must have been a pleasant job, for Lonsdale is here at its most majestic and beautiful. Surrounded by hills which slope down to rich pastures, settlements such as Arkholme developed on the Lune which offered a natural water supply, defence and the most effective transport route in the Middle Ages.

The bluff is known as Chapel Hill and is the oldest part of Arkholme. Anglo-Saxon settlers may have occupied this mound even before the Normans came and built their defensive 'motte and bailey' (moat and enclosure) stronghold. Similar

FOOD and DRINK

Many a farmer's tale must have been told by the log fire in the cosy wood panelled rooms of the Bay Horse, a traditional local overlooking the village crossroads. Stuffed animal heads and old photos of Arkholme remind you that you are in the wilds of the rural north country and here you can choose from a good selection of full meals, snacks, salads and sandwiches and wash your food down with Mitchell's Original Bitter. Meals are available both at lunchtimes and in the evening. Telephone: 01524 221425.

earthworks exist on the opposite side of the river at Melling and a ferry once operated from Arkholme linking the two settlements. The 15th-century John the Baptist church now occupies Chapel Hill but probably replaced a much older place of worship. From here, Arkholme developed as a straggling street running towards the 'high road' to Kirkby Lonsdale.

The walk starts at the village crossroads and follows paths through rolling pastures along the western flanks of the Lune valley before entering fields near Storrs Hall. The route continues along field paths through undulating countryside to arrive at a magnificent view of the river Lune on a steep spur above Loyn Bridge. From here the way back to Arkholme's old church is along the riverside, following the bank of the Lune upstream with distant views of Bowland and the Pennines.

THE WALK

❶   Begin the walk at the village crossroads by the Bay Horse. Facing the pub,

The Lune valley.

turn left and follow the pavement along the main road out of the village. Follow the roadside for about 250 yards until you reach a footpath leaving the road on the right-hand side. This is not the footpath signed to Locka Lane, but is further along than this and is reached after the pavement becomes a grass verge and the Wesleyan chapel (1890) is passed on the left-hand side of the road. Immediately after the chapel you will see the narrow metal stile to your right.

❷ Cross the stile and follow the way-marked path along the boundary around the farm buildings to your left. Further stiles are crossed and when you enter the large field at the rear of the buildings veer left and walk to the far side of the field. On reaching a clump of trees, go through the gateway in the field corner. Veer slightly right and walk through the next

field, keeping a tree-lined stream on your left. A footbridge is reached; cross this to arrive at the bottom of a field which rises steeply uphill.

❸ Go directly uphill towards trees and a white farmhouse comes into view. Head towards the farmhouse and cross the stile at the top of the hill which leads into another field. Walk alongside the boundary, crossing over another stile, to reach a brown gate alongside the farmhouse. Go through the gate and follow the driveway around to your left past other cottages and Locka Old Hall.

❹ The driveway leads out to Locka Lane. Turn left and follow this for over ¼ mile until it meets the main Carnforth-Kirkby Lonsdale road. Turn right and take care crossing the busy road to follow the grass verge for about 180 yards. Shortly after the private entrance to Storrs Hall is passed look for a small green gate in the wall to your left. Go through the gate, the route is signposted for Gressingham and Loyn Bridge.

❺ The fenced path leads through woodland and crosses a stile to enter parkland. Take the path that forks left and head straight through the trees with the grounds of Storrs Hall to your left. Cross a footbridge over a stream and follow the path over another stile to enter a large field. Walk straight ahead in the direction of woodland and at the far side of the field a gate is reached.

❻ Go through the gate and walk over the enclosure, passing through further gates to

---

PLACES of INTEREST

Less than 1½ miles along the lane which leads north from the crossroads by the Bay Horse is **Docker Park Farm**, an ideal family attraction centred around a working animal farm. There are demonstrations and exhibitions as well as a chance to feed the various animals, view the rare breeds and walk around the trout lakes. Telephone: 01524 221331. Continue along the B6254 for 5 miles from the Arkholme crossroads to arrive at the Cumbrian market town of **Kirkby Lonsdale** nestling amidst the beautiful scenery of the Lune valley. There is an excellent viewpoint along the river Lune – which is easily accessible from the town centre. The street is lined with numerous pubs and gift shops leading to the old square, where a traditional market is regularly held. For Kirkby Lonsdale Tourist Information, telephone 01524 271437.

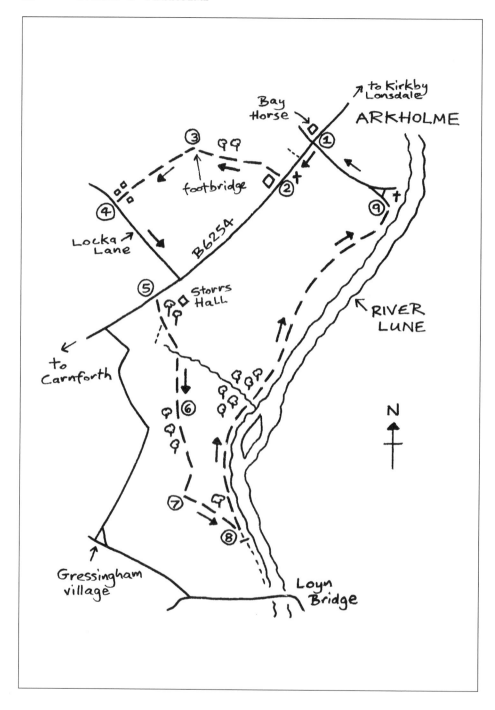

enter a hedged square field. Walk diagonally downhill to another gate in the opposite field corner. From here turn right and walk along the field edge which climbs uphill, turn left at the field corner and continue alongside the hedge boundary to reach a stile at the top of the field. Cross the stile and take in the magnificent views of the Lune valley and the Bowland hills.

❼ From the stile drop downhill, veering slightly right, heading in the direction of the farm buildings which can be seen on the opposite side of the river. Below the steep spur of the hill, the riverside path is joined just before a gate is reached. Do not continue through the gate to Loyn Bridge but instead, turn sharp left and follow the riverside path upstream towards woodland.

❽ The path now follows a section of the longer 'Lune Valley Ramble' along the river bank for 1¼ miles back towards Arkholme. Stiles and footbridges are crossed as the track runs between a riverside line of trees and the boundaries of fields above the river bank. The track eventually leaves the riverside and enters a field via a stile. Follow the field edge to return to the river embankment. The path through the riverside pasture leads towards a stile in the field corner alongside woodland.

❾ Cross the stile and join the lane which heads uphill. This leads directly back to the village centre but, before returning, turn right up the first little alleyway and then right again to explore the medieval church of St John the Baptist. The church, restored in the 1890s, stands upon the ancient site of Chapel Hill and has the remains of a cross – possibly of Saxon origin – in its grounds. From the church go back down the alley and rejoin the main lane. Turn right here and walk back to the village crossroads.

BOLTON-LE-SANDS

Length: 4½ miles

Getting there: The village straddles the A6, 4 miles north of Lancaster and 2 miles south of Carnforth. But leave the A6 along a minor road to reach the village centre which is on	the east side of the main road. **Parking:** Along the main village street or by the picnic area which is down St	Michael's Lane, next to the Lancaster Canal. **Map:** OS Landranger 97 Kendal to Morecambe (GR 484678).

As you travel along the A6 road north of Lancaster, Bolton-le-Sands appears to be nothing more than an uninteresting ribbon of post-war suburban housing. But, in fact, 'Boelton's' recorded history begins with the granting of an 11th-century place of worship upon whose ancient foundations the present Holy Trinity parish church now stands. The church has a 15th-century tower, a familiar landmark which guided fishermen and cockle pickers back to the shore from the hazardous Morecambe Bay mud-flats.

Since the late 18th century transport developments began to transform the ancient settlement. First, the bumpy old road between Lancaster and Kendal was turnpiked in 1754, then the Lancaster Canal opened in 1797. The canal enjoyed a brief 'golden age' before the railway link between Lancaster and Carlisle was completed in 1846 and the modern M6, a mile to the east of the village, completes the picture.

Starting from the village centre by the church of St Mary of the Angels, the walk follows the secluded Lancaster Canal south to Hest Bank, then crosses the A6 and the railway to return along Morecambe Bay's muddy shores – ideal for birdwatching. Along the shoreline section of this walk do not stray from the path as Morecambe Bay is infamous for its fast rising tides – so please take heed of the warning notices.

THE WALK

❶ Leave the main village street by turning down St Michael's Lane which is almost opposite the church of St Mary of the Angels (dating from 1884). The lane goes

past the Old School and St Michael's Cottage before crossing over a canal bridge. Turn left and go down the steps to join the towpath of the Lancaster Canal which linked the towns of North Lancashire and Westmorland with the Leeds-Liverpool Canal and the Wigan coalfield. The northern terminus was Kendal though this section did not open until 1819.

❷ Follow the towpath directly ahead for just over 1 mile. The canal passes under the A6 road and meanders between handsome suburban properties before passing under a stone bridge, number 118, close to the Hest Bank pub. Beyond the bridge, leave the towpath by the canal signpost indicating 'village centre ¼ mile, shore ½ mile'. Take the steps to the right of the signpost and join Station Road.

❸ Go down Station Road and alongside shops cross the main Coastal Road via the pedestrian crossing. Then go over the high railway footbridge to join the Lancashire Coastal Way which follows the lane past the Shore Cafe.

❹ Beyond the car parking area the lane

A view of Warton Crag across Morecambe Bay.

becomes a track; keep to this and follow the shoreline to reach another car parking area close to a farm. From here the path runs alongside a stone wall and then reaches a stone stile in a wall next to a Lancashire Coastal Way signpost.

❺ Cross over the stile and climb up through the hillside field to gain excellent views south to the resort of Morecambe and north to Warton Crag and the more distant Lakeland Fells. The path then drops down to a stile which leads into a small caravan site. Cross the stile and veer left around the caravans to reach a stone stile in a narrow gap between a wall and farm buildings. Cross over the stile and pass Red Bank Farm on the right.

❻ From the farm keep to the coastal path for nearly ¾ mile. Part of the route follows an embankment running parallel to a lane lined with cottages but continue along the shore after the lane turns sharp right up a hill until another lane is reached which follows the shoreline towards farm buildings.

❼ On joining this lane, close to a 'Danger' notice, turn right and leave the coastal path. Follow the lane uphill, passing a mill and crossing over the railway. Continue along the main avenue (Mill Lane) until the busy A6 is reached.

❽ Turn right and follow the pavement along the main road past the Royal Hotel and cross the A6 safely via the pedestrian crossing, reached just before a petrol sta-

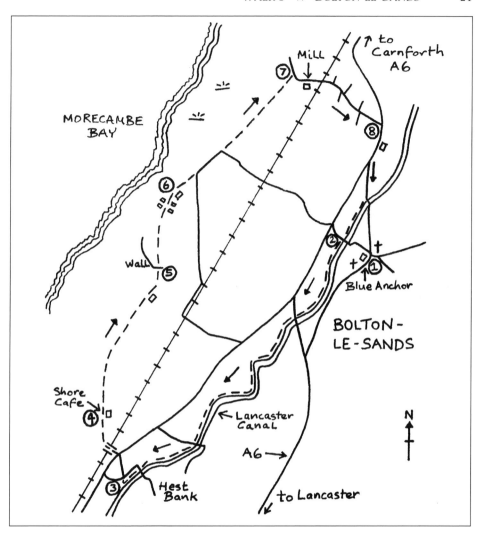

tion. Then turn left up Main Road which leads uphill to reach the canal. Turn right and rejoin the canal towpath via steps. Continue straight ahead and after passing under the next bridge, number 122, go up the steps to rejoin St Michael's Lane. A short walk up the hill brings you back into the old village centre. Continue down the main street past the Blue Anchor to explore Holy Trinity church.

WALK 4

GLASSON

Length: 5 miles

Getting there: Glasson is situated upon the Lune estuary, 4 miles south-west of Lancaster. Approach the village via the A588 between Lancaster and the village of Cockerham, continuing along the B5290 which is signposted for Glasson by a bridge at the hamlet of Conder Green. If approaching on the M6, leave at junction 33.

Parking: There is a large car park (with a reasonable daily charge) at the East Quay which overlooks the marina.

Map: OS Landranger 102 Preston and Blackpool (GR 445561).

Did Glasson really once rival Liverpool as a great Lancashire port? It is hard to believe, but goods from the West Indies and timber from Canada were being imported to the village even before Liverpool had begun to enjoy its great Victorian heyday as Britain's chief Atlantic port.

Lancaster merchants invested in Glasson and a dock was opened here in 1791 – claiming to be the first wet dock in Lancashire! Movement of raw materials and goods in and out was further facilitated when a branch of the Lancaster Canal reached Glasson in 1826, with a waterway linking the dock to the canal basin.

The tiny cluster of farmsteads that had clung to the shore here since medieval times were thus transformed as Glasson Dock became a thriving quayside. Rows of sturdy terraces sprang up to house dock workers now employed in new industries far removed from the traditions of farming and fishing. But agriculture has always remained an important part of the village's economy – not so surprising, as the vast expanse of low-lying natural mossland hereabouts was drained and improved even by the early 19th century, creating a fertile land ripe for crops and dairy farming.

This walk starts at the East Quay car park and climbs out of the village heading for the sea. Quiet lanes and paths lead across Thurnham Moss to the lonely shore with the desolate Cockersand Abbey overlooking the sluggish channel where the river Lune meets the Irish Sea. From here the walk follows the Lancashire Coastal Way long-distance path back to the village. From the shore there are extensive views north and east to the City of Lancaster and the high Bowland Fells. Look

out in particular for the green dome of Lancaster's Ashton Memorial and the bright white campus of the city's university.

THE WALK

❶ From the car park overlooking the marina turn left to cross the waterway over the road which connects the marina and the dock. The boating marina occupies the basin of the Glasson branch of the Lancaster Canal. Continue straight ahead up the main village street (Thurnham Terrace) and at the road junction on the brow of Tithe Barn Hill turn left by the viewpoint indicator to go down the hill, following the pavement. When the road swings sharp left continue straight ahead, crossing over to join the lane signed as a no through road.

❷ Follow the lane for nearly ½ a mile, passing Old Glasson Farm, until you reach a gate on the right alongside the driveway entrance to Kendal Hill Farm. Leave the lane here, go through the gate and follow the signed public footpath along the track between fields. After 300 yards, just before the track starts to bend to the left, look for the gate on the right-hand side and go through this.

❸ From the gate go directly across the field to another gate. Go through this and continue straight ahead past derelict farm buildings and continue in the same direction through the field with the hedge boundary immediately to your right. Follow the field edge until shortly you pass through two gates in the corner of the field to reach a lane.

❹ Turn right and follow the lane past farmhouses. Keep to the lane and after nearly a mile it zig-zags around to a junction with another lane signposted for Cockersand Abbey car park. However, ignore this lane and fork left along the lane which zig-zags for nearly ½ mile until a track entering Cockersand Abbey Farm is reached on your right. The landscape walked through here is typical of the extensive mosslands which were formed naturally between the low-lying valleys of the rivers Wyre and Lune.

❺ Leave the lane here and take the footpath which leads up past deserted farm buildings to reach the remains of Cockersand Abbey where there is an information board. For medieval monks seeking solitude there could have been few sites more ideal than this windy promontory upon

The remains of 13th-century Cockersand Abbey.

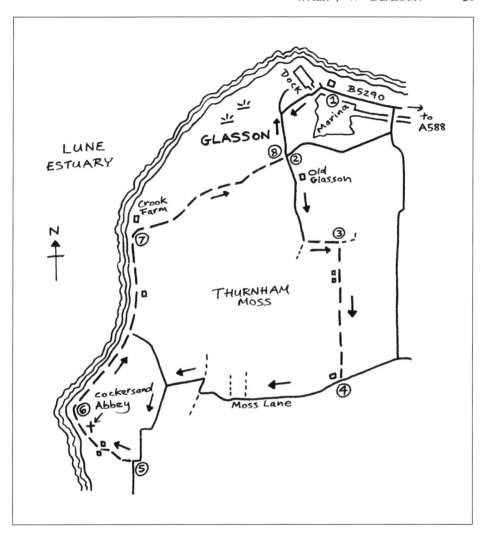

which was originally established a 12th-century hermitage by Hugh Garth. The site became a 13th-century abbey of the strict Premonstratensian order and the monks were known to catch fresh salmon in the Lune tides. The abbey light was also a useful navigational beacon for shipping. All that remains of the abbey now is the sandstone chapter house which became the burial vault of the Dalton family who resided at nearby Thurnham Hall.

❻ From the abbey continue towards the sea, pass through a kissing gate and join the coastal footpath. This route is part of the Lancashire Coastal Way long-distance footpath. Turn right and follow the path around the promontory, heading towards the distant Heysham Power Station. Out to sea, the nearby lighthouse beacon guides boats up the winding channel of the Lune Estuary. Continue along the embankment wall, passing the small abbey car park and cottages until the path leaves the shore in front of Crook Farm.

❼ Go down the track in front of the farm buildings, passing through two gates to join a muddy track between hedges. Go through another gate and continue along the track which crosses a footbridge and leads to a hedged lane. Walk along the lane, passing Old Glasson caravan park on your right, and shortly it arrives back at the public road close to where you left it near the start of the walk.

❽ Turn left, cross over to the pavement and retrace your steps up and down the hill back to Glasson. Despite some obvious 20th century 'suburban' housing development, Glasson's terraced rows date mainly from the 19th century and were associated with the rise of the port of Glasson, itself linked with the opening of the Lancaster Canal and later a railway connection to the city. The dock is still active but pleasure boats now dominate the canal basin – adding a touch of colourful holiday glamour to Glasson's industrial scene.

SLAIDBURN

Length: 5½ miles

Getting there: The village is situated on the B6478, 8 miles north of Clitheroe.	toilets and picnic area are situated alongside the B6478 between the village centre and Slaidburn Bridge. The car park	**Map:** OS Landranger 103 Blackburn and Burnley (GR 712525).
Parking: A free public car park,	is well signposted.	

Prior to boundary changes in 1974 Slaidburn was in Yorkshire, but Lancastrians can overlook such a blemish for this chunk of Bowland is a most picturesque addition to the county. The stone cottages lining the roadside between the bridge over the river Hodder and the 13th-century church of St Andrew hark back to medieval times when Slaidburn was the administrative centre of the Royal Forest of Bowland. Here forest tenants came to pay their rents and a manorial court was housed in an upper room of what is now the village inn. Time has thankfully stood still amidst Slaidburn's cobbled streets and much of the village is now part of a conservation area.

FOOD and DRINK

No visit to Slaidburn is complete without a look at the Hark to Bounty, probably the most famous Bowland inn. Ramblers and youth hostellers now congregate in the stone rooms above which is the preserved medieval court room where disputes were settled in the Forest of Bowland. The hostelry was formerly known as the Dog Inn until the 1870s, but then the present unusual name came into use – it being the legendary exclamation of a Reverend Wigglesworth who was sitting in the inn one particular hunting day and heard his favourite pack hound, Bounty, baying outside. You may hear many such old yarns in the Hark to Bounty if you hang around long enough. Needless to say, good food and ales are provided here. Telephone: 01200 446246.

There is much of interest here: the old church, the 18th-century grammar school, 17th-century farmhouses, the Hark to Bounty inn, the youth hostel – formerly the Black Bull – the imposing war memorial and Victoria's Jubilee Well in addition to numerous 19th-century buildings. Surrounding Slaidburn is excellent walking country, from the high Bowland Fells to the lush pastures of the river Hodder which flows south through the village on its way to join the river Ribble near Hurst Green. The mightiest Lancashire river rising in Yorkshire – perish the thought!

This walk starts at the village car park close to Slaidburn Bridge and heads south along riverside paths and lanes, following the course of the river Hodder downstream past historic farmhouses to the neighbouring village of Newton. Newton itself is worth exploring, after which the walk returns through pastures along the opposite side of the river, passing along the way the spooky towers of abandoned Dunnow Hall.

THE WALK

❶ From the car park head towards the river Hodder by taking the public footpath which is signposted alongside the stone Methodist chapel. This leads onto a riverside path beneath trees and very shortly two kissing gates are reached.

❷ Ignore the first kissing gate, but go through the second – the route ahead is signposted as a permissive riverside path; this has been provided by permission of the owner so please keep to the way-marked path along the river bank. Several stiles are crossed as the path heads down the valley. Follow the riverside for about ½ mile, after which the path reaches a sewage works fence and swings sharp right, away from the river, crossing stiles and a little footbridge to reach a track.

❸ Turn left onto the track, go through the gateway to the sewage works then turn left to follow the permissive path which runs down the opposite side of the sewage works fence and rejoins the river. Continue along the riverside for a further ¼ mile until the path rejoins the track by an old bridge.

❹ Cross the bridge over the river but do not follow the obvious track. Instead go directly towards an old footbridge and iron kissing gate which can be glimpsed on the far side of the field. Go through the kissing gate which leads into a large field. Cross the field, veering slightly to the left of the farm buildings which can be seen directly ahead on the opposite side of the field. Look out for another iron kissing gate with railings in the corner of the field and go through it. Walk along the field edge with the fence to your right and, after a short distance, pass through a gate which leads out onto a lane opposite a farmhouse.

❺ Turn right and follow the lane past the buildings of Robinson's Farm – which have a date stone of 1699. Continue along the lane for nearly ¾ mile as it meanders over a little stream and begins to climb uphill to reach a signpost in a hedge which indicates public footpaths beginning on either side of the lane.

❻ Take the footpath on the right-hand side of the lane by going through the gate and following the track which leads downhill between fields. The track soon peters out when it enters a narrow field with a stone barn to your right. Walk downhill through the narrow field, keeping to the left-hand edge of the field alongside trees. Note the good views back up the valley from here and at the bottom corner of the field cross over a stone step stile by a gate.

❼ Veer left to rejoin the river. Cross the field to reach a stone stile and gate just to the left of Newton Bridge. Join the road here and turn right, crossing the bridge over the river to explore the little village of Newton – interesting buildings include Newton Hall, Newton National School (1842), the Georgian Parkers Arms and numerous 17th-century farmhouses.

❽ From the village retrace your steps downhill back to Newton Bridge. But do not cross the river, instead join the path along the near side of the river by going through the wooden gate in the wall next

to the road. Go down steps to join the stone paved path which clings closely to the riverside. The waymarked route leads through fields and crosses stiles, eventually reaching a stile in a field corner by the river. Cross this and follow the path through woodland to reach an iron kissing gate. Go through this and continue directly across the field to join the track to the left of the bridge crossed earlier in this walk.

❾ Turn left onto the track and follow it back up the valley, passing the gothic towers of Dunnow Hall in woodland to your left. The Hall was built in the 1830s for the local Wilkinson family. After re-passing the sewage works rejoin the riverside path followed earlier in this walk. Retrace your steps along the river, crossing stiles, but after passing through the first kissing gate take an alternative route back to the village by going through the adjacent kissing gate to your left.

PLACES of INTEREST

Signposted from the centre of Slaidburn and just 1½ miles to the north is **Myttons Farm Craft Centre** where hand painted pottery is made on the premises. Pick up some unique gifts here and as well as a shop there is also a tea room. Telephone: 01200 446200. Head north from Slaidburn along the B6478 (crossing over Slaidburn Bridge) and within a few miles take the minor lane turning to the left which leads to **Stocks Reservoir** and **Gisburn Forest**. There is parking alongside the vast moorland reservoir from where you can admire the views and even continue your walking along the trails through the forest.

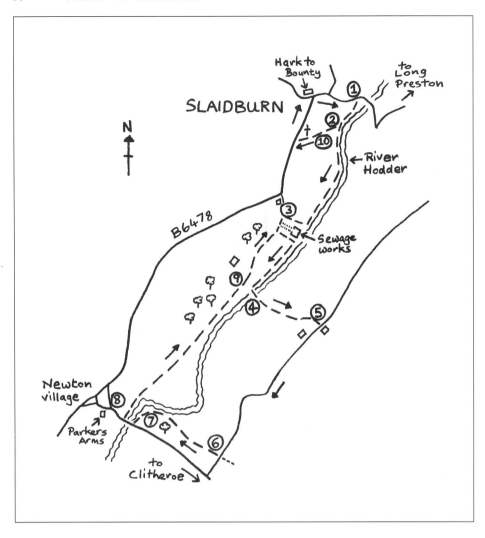

⑩ From this kissing gate walk diagonally across the field towards the nearby church. Another kissing gate leads into the yard of St Andrew's which is worth exploring. From the church the right of way continues to the lane. Turn right along the lane to walk back through Slaidburn village, passing 17th-century farmhouses. When the Hark to Bounty pub is reached turn right down the lane, passing the impressive war memorial, to shortly reach the car park on the left-hand side of the road.

SCORTON

Length: 4 miles

Getting there: The village is situated between the A6 and M6, 2 miles north of Garstang. The nearest junction on the M6 is junction 33, from here follow the A6 south and turn off at the minor lane signposted to Scorton.	Parking: Parking places are limited in the small village. There are spaces opposite the village stores in front of the Priory Restaurant (not the Priory's car park which is to the rear) and a few spaces in front of the Methodist church which	are not available during the times of services. Map: OS Landranger 102 Preston and Blackpool (GR 502488).

Shady Scorton is easily overlooked in the great north-south rush of traffic hurtling along the A6, M6 and railway between Preston and Lancaster. Yet all three transport corridors are just a stone's throw from the village post office. Indeed, both the

motorway and the railway have had to kink to the east and west of Scorton to accommodate the village, so protecting its unspoilt cottages, leafy lanes and 19th-century churches. Nestling between the valley of the river Wyre and the foothills

FOOD and DRINK

Thirsty walkers who have tackled the slopes of Nicky Nook must not despair over the lack of village pub for the Priory is close at hand. This popular tea room-cum-restaurant has a licensed bar and large rooms arranged around a shop where gifts and cakes can be bought. There is plenty of choice, from snacks to three course meals, ranging from simple poached egg on toast to steaks and starters such as Morecambe Bay potted shrimps on brown toast. There is also a colourful array of delicious home-made desserts. The Priory is open all day everyday. Telephone: 01524 791255.

of Bowland, Scorton may also be over-looked by visitors for another reason – it has no village pub!

Religion and work have shaped the traditional social life of this community. John Wesley preached in the village in the 18th century and opposite the tree where he stood, a Wesleyan chapel was estab-lished by local mill owner George Fishwick in 1842. Two other places of wor-ship were erected in the 19th century – St Mary and St James' Catholic church and the Anglican church of St Peter with its tall spire. The Priory, now a restaurant, was once the home of the local Catholic priest. Meanwhile, the Fishwick Brothers came from Burnley in 1809 and set up a short-lived cotton spinning enterprise in the village.

This walk is best completed on a fine clear day when the spectacular views from the top of Nicky Nook can be enjoyed to their fullest. Starting by the Priory restau-rant the walk leaves Scorton along Tithe Barn Lane which climbs eastwards, cross-ing under the M6, and leads to the secluded valley of Grizedale. A wooded

track up the valley is followed as far as Grizedale Reservoir, from where the path ascends steeply to the prominent hilltop of Nicky Nook which provides one of the finest views across Lancashire. The path drops down from here to join Snowhill Lane which leads back over the motorway to the village.

THE WALK

❶ From the Priory restaurant walk along the main village street southwards in the direction of the Methodist chapel (with an 1842 date stone). Continue until the vil-lage bowling club is passed on the left, behind which is the tall spire of St Peter's church. Immediately after passing the bowling green turn left up Tithe Barn Lane.

❷ The lane climbs quite steeply under the motorway bridge and swings right then left past houses. Keep to the lane for about ½ mile and eventually it climbs to a T-junction with another lane. Turn right onto this lane and follow it for a further ¼ mile. Shortly after farmhouses are passed on the right the road begins to drop down-hill, at which point a track will be seen

PLACES of INTEREST

The traditional market town of **Garstang** is worth a look and is just 2 miles south of Scorton along the A6. Garstang's attractions include its Thursday market and the **Discovery Centre** which is on High Street. Here displays and exhibitions chart the history and heritage of the Wyre district and the centre also provides comprehensive tourist infor-mation on other Lancashire attractions. Telephone: 01995 602125.

The summit of Nicky Nook with its wide views of the county.

forking off to the left of the road – signposted 'Grizedale valley'.

❸ Leave the road and go through the gate to follow the track down the wooded hillside. At the bottom of the hill turn right and go over the field to cross a stile on the left-hand side of a gate.

❹ Turn left here and follow the bridle track which runs along the left-hand side of Grizedale Brook. Follow the main track through secluded woodland below moors for about a mile until Grizedale Reservoir is reached on the right beyond a kissing gate. Walk alongside the reservoir wall for a further 400 yards until a footpath signpost is reached on the left. Look out for the steps which lead over the wall to the

left along the footpath signposted 'Nicky Nook for Scorton 1½ miles'.

❺ Climb up the steps and over the wall. The ascent up the well-trodden path now begins – but take a rest on the memorial bench a little further up the steep hill. At the top of the hill the land flattens out to a moorland plateau. Do not take the well-trodden path which forks left from here but instead follow the path which is closer to the wall on your right. By a gate in the wall veer left away from it to cross the moor – the path is quickly joined by another path coming from a ladder stile in the wall to your right. The distinct path through the grass leads slightly uphill to reach a white triangulation pillar on the summit of Nicky Nook.

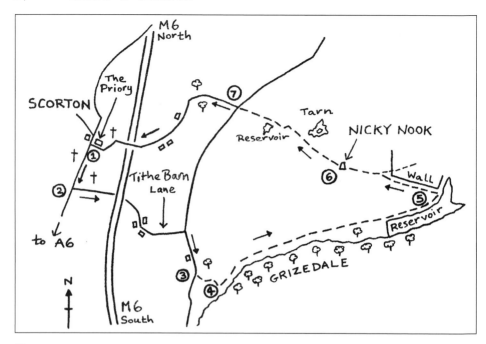

❻ Admire the view from here which stretches in all directions to cover a vast sweep of Lancashire from the Bowland hills in the east to Blackpool and Morecambe Bay in the west, from the Lake District in the north to the West Pennines in the south. To continue the walk head in the direction of Morecambe Bay, passing a summit cairn and following a distinct path in the grass which veers right and drops gradually downhill towards a tarn and a group of stunted conifers. The curious windblown trees by the tarn on the top of Nicky Nook are a familiar landmark from the M6 below. The path goes through a gap in the wall and then through a kissing gate by a tiny reservoir. Continue the steep descent to a kissing gate at a lane.

❼ Continue the downward descent by joining the lane on the opposite side to the kissing gate. This lane (Snowhill Lane) eventually crosses the motorway bridge. The busy M6 is a world far removed from the seclusion of Grizedale. After the motorway the lane drops steeply down to Scorton, passing the church of St Mary and St James, the village school and the war memorial cross before arriving back at the Priory.

KNOTT END-ON-SEA

Length: 4¾ miles

Getting there: Knott End is situated at the end of the B5270, 1 mile north-west of Preesall village. Approach it via the A588 Lancaster-Poulton road and turn off for Preesall, following the signposts to Knott End.

Parking: There is free parking along the Esplanade or in the Quail Holme Road car park just behind the Coastguard Station and Knott End Cafe.

Map: OS Landranger 102 Preston and Blackpool (GR 347486).

Knott End-on-Sea is a quaint seaside backwater which is literally at the end of the line. The road ends here above the sands running down to the deep channel of the river Wyre. A railway line from Garstang once ended here and along with it the ambitious plans of Victorian entrepreneurs to transform Knott End into a great railway port. These days the neat avenues and well kept gardens of suburban bungalows house many retired Lancastrians who have come in search of fresh air and gentle strolls along the prom.

But Knott End's isolation has helped it to maintain its charm. Bordered on two sides by the sea and river, inland the village is surrounded by vast acres of reclaimed mossland and tiny rural settlements. Only the seasonal ferry crossing to Fleetwood appears to link the village with modern urban life. Yet centuries before the port of Fleetwood was born, the Wyre estuary was the haunt of Norse invaders and night time smugglers who weaved in and out of the mud flats and creeks.

The walk starts at the free car park behind the Coastguard Station. From here, the coastal path along the sea embankment is followed for a few miles before turning inland to reach the hilltop village of Preesall. The route then heads back to the coast along tracks to arrive at secluded Hackensall Hall. The walk ends by following the estuary path back to Knott End, offering views across the river to the port of Fleetwood and Blackpool Tower.

THE WALK

❶ From the free car park behind the Coastguard Station walk towards the Bourne Arms Hotel and follow the pavement along the Esplanade. When the road bends right to the village shops leave it and continue straight ahead past the viewpoint indicator. Follow the well-used tarmac path which follows the sea

defences between houses and the shore. The houses end in fields and a caravan park is passed on your right. Immediately after passing a second caravan park – Sandy Bay – look out for a set of concrete steps to your right.

❷ Leave the shore by going down the steps and follow the path between the drain and the caravans which leads to the driveway of the Sandy Bay site. Very shortly a residential lane is reached. Cross the lane and slightly to the left join the signed footpath on the opposite side of the road. Follow the field path with the drain and boundary to your immediate right. Further stiles are crossed before two footbridges are reached and you continue straight ahead from here, crossing further stiles to join a farm track.

❸ Turn left along the track and follow it as it winds between buildings. The track veers right and becomes a residential lane (Little Tongues Lane). At the junction with the main road alongside the garage,

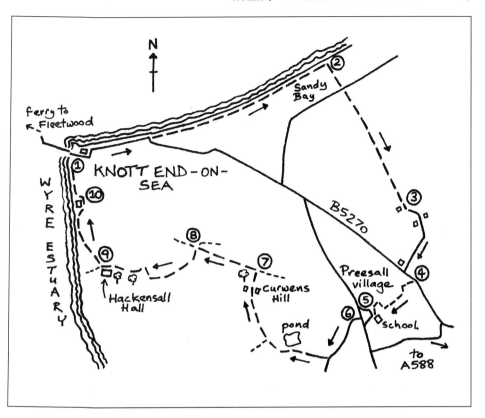

turn left and follow the pavement along the main road. Take care – as the pavement soon gives way to a narrow verge. Follow the road for about 200 yards, passing Gaulter's Lane on the left and then cross to reach a stile next to a bus stop.

❹ Cross the stile and follow the field path over stiles to a footbridge at the bottom of a steep hill. Climb directly up the hill to arrive at a stile in front of Preesall's village school.

❺ Turn right and follow the enclosed path around the school site to emerge by the school entrance. Walk down the driveway to join a lane. Turn right along the lane which winds down to the village centre. Go through the alleyway between the Round House and the post office to join the main road. Take care and cross the main road to join Back Lane which begins to the left of the pub. Preesall still has an old rural charm even though it is no stranger to industrial development – for instance, a railway (now disused) and salt mines along the coast.

❻ Follow Back Lane for nearly ¼ mile until the junction with another lane on the right – signed as Acker's Lane. Turn right and follow Acker's Lane; the lane

The hilltop village of Preesall visited on the walk.

eventually becomes a track and you continue along it beyond the 'Private Road – Footpath Only' sign. The farm track leads past a fishing pond and reaches a footpath signpost highlighting the junction of three paths. You may be able to spot Blackpool Tower from here! Continue in the same direction along the route signposted for Curwens Hill. The track leads gradually uphill and bends right to reach farm buildings. At the end of the track look for a stile in the wall to your right and cross it to enter a field. Follow the field edge beneath the trees, dropping down the hill to reach an old metal kissing gate in the field corner.

❼ From the kissing gate turn left to follow a track between hedges. This track is actually part of a disused railway line which ran from Knott End to Garstang and was used mainly for the movement of farm produce. The line was known to locals as the 'Pilling Pig' after the engine's distinctive whistle. This section opened in 1908 and was closed as early as 1950. Continue along the straight track for about ¼ mile until you reach a crossroads of paths at the start of a small wood. A path leads directly ahead beneath the trees, but there are also paths to the left and right.

❽ Turn sharp left here and take the wide hedged track which runs towards a farmhouse. The track swings right and heads towards woodland. The lane meanders into the woodland and you should ignore the tracks which join it on the right and left. A signpost is reached indicating 'Knott End ¾ mile'; continue in this direction passing the presently derelict Hackensall Hall – the 17th-century buildings replaced an older manorial house. Follow the track through a gateway to your right and walk with the buildings to your left. At the end of the buildings look out for the waymarker post.

❾ Turn right here and follow the waymarked path – signposted as the Wyre Way – along a hedge until another signpost is reached by a pond. Leave the hedge side here and veer left, walking diagonally across the golf links. Beware of the danger of driven golf balls here. Head towards the old wooden garage and electricity poles on the opposite side of the fairway. At the garage turn right and follow the track which runs between the shore cliffs and the golf links. Follow the waymarkers which lead around the side of Sea Dyke Cottage. Pass this on the left then turn immediately left to join the sea wall.

❿ Turn right and follow the sea wall back in the direction of the ferry pier and the sea. The Coastguard Station is soon reached on your left alongside the Knott End Cafe. Further along the promenade road is the Bourne Arms Hotel. If returning to the car park, turn right after the Knott End Cafe to go down Quail Holme Road.

CHIPPING

Length: 4 miles

Getting there: The village is best approached from Longridge which is 6 miles north-east of Preston and reached by the B5269 or the B6243. Chipping is 4 miles further north and is signposted from Longridge town centre.

Parking: There is a free car park in the village. Adjacent to this is an overflow coach and car park.

Maps: OS Landranger 102 Preston and Blackpool or 103 Blackburn and Burnley (GR 622433).

Nestling between hills along back roads miles from anywhere has not been enough to protect Chipping from coach loads of tourists eager to sample the delights of one of Lancashire's most perfect villages. In fact, Chipping has never been a sleepy backwater, for even in medieval times it was the chief market centre for a wide rural area stretching from the Bowland Fells down to the valley of the river Hodder. The waters of Chipping Brook powered corn mills until the 18th and 19th centuries, and new industrial enterprises were attracted to the fast-flowing stream bringing the bustle of chair-making, cotton spinning and iron working to Chipping's winding lanes.

Chippingers have had some reward

FOOD and DRINK

The three village pubs in close proximity in the centre of the village are all worth trying – the Sun Inn, the Talbot and the Tillotson's Arms are all cosy and cater for the visitor with food and fine ales. The prominent Sun Inn with its stone staircase entrance holds the most commanding position overlooking Windy Street and its many rooms surrounding its small bar are the haunt of local ghost Lizzie Dean. She may tap you on the shoulder whilst you are drinking Boddingtons or enjoying a ploughman's, pie or the inn's famous Lancashire 'cheese bombs'. Telephone: 01995 61206. Also, on the corner near the car park is the Cobbled Corner Cafe, popular with cyclists and coach parties. Telephone: 01995 61551.

though – for the village is no stranger to winning Best Kept Village competitions! This would no doubt have pleased local cloth dealer John Brabyn whose 17th-century home, almshouses and school are some of the main features of interest in the village. In addition, there is the restored medieval church, St Bartholomew's, which stands sentinel at the top of the village's main street, a church where many great Lancashire landowners came to worship.

Starting from the village car park, this walk offers a taste of the Bowland Fells and highlights the contrast between the rugged moorland to the north of Chipping and the lush valley pastures to the south of the village. The walk leads past the famous Berry's Chair Works and follows field paths to reach the lower slopes of the distinctive hump-backed hill of Parlick. From here there are fine views looking south across the Loud valley towards Pendle Hill and Longridge Fell. Field paths and lanes lead back to the village centre.

THE WALK

❶ Begin the walk on the church side of the car park, turning left to walk along the lane signed as Church Rake. Walk up the lane and shortly after passing houses it forks. Take the right fork which leads downhill and uphill past the Chair Works and mill pond. The 19th-century Chair Works was originally powered by the water of the stream. Opposite the mill pond look out for a stile on the right-hand side of the lane alongside the gate to Austin House.

❷ Cross the stile and follow the footpath uphill through the field. Another stile is crossed, shortly after which a waymarker post indicates a fork in the path in the middle of a field. Follow the left fork, dropping slightly downhill to woodland. Cross another stile between trees and the path veers left through woodland to cross a high footbridge. Turn right after the footbridge and head uphill towards a stone cottage (which has an 1860 date stone).

❸ Just to the left of the gate alongside the cottage join the stone track and turn left. Follow the track downhill to a stream and

woodland and then uphill to join a minor lane beyond a gate. Cross the lane and go directly ahead, following the farm road uphill towards Saddle End. Just before reaching the farm buildings look out for a stile on the left-hand side of the farm road which leads into a woodland plantation. Note the fine views south revealing Pendle Hill and Longridge Fell.

❹ Cross this stile and follow the meandering path between trees. At the edge of the wood cross another stile and continue in the same direction across a marshy field heading towards the magnificent moorland spur of Parlick. Cross further stiles and head directly towards the farmhouse, the field falls away to reveal a steep sided valley. Follow the path down to the foot-

The path leading to the prominent spur of Parlick.

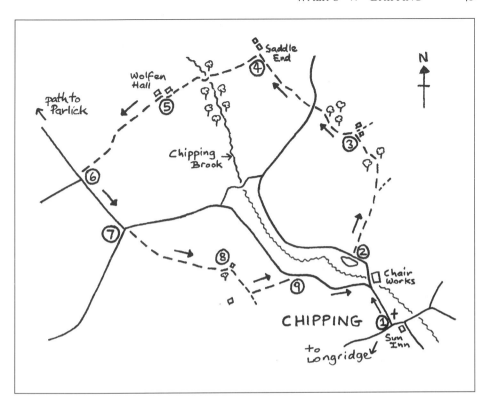

bridges at the stream bottom (Chipping Brook) and then climb out of the valley, crossing another stile to shortly arrive at the farm (Wolfen Hall).

❺ Go through a waymarked gate on the right after passing the first buildings and turn immediately left to join the farm road. Cross a cattle grid and follow the farm road uphill. Follow this for nearly ½ mile until a minor lane is reached.

❻ Turn left and follow the lane downhill. Go directly ahead along the lane for more than ¼ mile until a T-junction is reached.

❼ On the far side of the junction cross the stile and join the footpath which leads through a field alongside a wall. The path soon veers left downhill alongside the line of the wall – head for the woodland below. At the bottom of the hill cross a stile and go directly ahead to cross a little stream in the field corner. Turn right and follow the field edge alongside the stream, heading towards a barn. Just before the barn is reached cross the stream again by some stepping stones to reach a stone stile.

❽ Cross the stile over the wall and go directly ahead to reach a stile in the corner of the small field. Cross this and head for the stile clearly visible on the far side of the field. Cross this to join a farm

PLACES of INTEREST

Why not explore the Forest of Bowland more intimately by visiting **Browsholme Hall**, the ancestral home of the Parker family who were traditionally the keepers of the forest's deer park. The Hall is Tudor in origin and its remarkable collection of artefacts gives an insight into the way of life in a medieval hunting forest. Browsholme Hall is only 5 miles from Chipping by road. Follow the lane towards Clitheroe and brown tourist signs point the way; the Hall is just north of the hamlet of Bashall Eaves. Telephone: 01254 826719. To admire the wild beauty of the Bowland Fells, follow the minor lanes out from Chipping which lead north via Whitewell and Dunsop Bridge to the famous moorland road leading over the **Trough Of Bowland**. This is the name given to the high pass in the hills carved by streams and the top of the pass is a popular viewpoint.

drive, turn left on the drive and then follow the field edge down to the adjoining lane.

❾ Turn right onto the lane and follow this downhill past cottages until shortly the lane swings right to join the road leading back into the village alongside St Bartholomew's church. Walk down the hill from the church to explore the village. The 17th-century buildings associated with cloth merchant John Brabyn are located in nearby Windy Street but there are many other interesting cottages if you go straight down the hill past the Tillotson's Arms to the bridge over Chipping Brook – where an old corn mill complete with water wheel has been imaginatively transformed into a restaurant.

GREAT ECCLESTON

Length: 2 miles

Getting there: The village is situated on the south side of the busy A586, roughly halfway between Poulton-le-Fylde and Garstang, and is signposted along a minor lane. If approach-ing via the motorway, leave the M55 at junction 3.

Parking: There is ample parking along the main village street and in the market square – but there are parking restrictions on market days (Wednesdays).

Map: OS Landranger 102 Preston and Blackpool (GR 402426).

The village dates back to the 11th-century Domesday Book when it was known as 'Egleston', the 'church town'. The prefix 'Great' was added to distinguish it from the adjoining hamlet of Little Eccleston less than a mile to the west. Situated in the heart of the Fylde plain, Great Eccleston was for many years an important market centre for the surrounding rural area and its square still holds a traditional weekly market. Many of the houses along the main thoroughfare date from the 18th and 19th centuries and fashionable travellers to the coast in Georgian times would stop here and mingle with Fylde folk. Now the holidaymakers come in cars and Great

Eccleston has cashed in on the passing trade along the busy route from Lancaster to the coast.

The river Wyre – a Celtic name translating as 'winding' – can be found just to the north of the village, lazily completing the last third of its circuitous journey from the Bowland Fells to the estuary at Fleetwood. The river has by now entered the flat drift plain of the Fylde which contrasts closely to the stark plateau of the Forest of Bowland to the east where the Wyre's adventure begins.

This short walk starts at the Market Square and leaves the village along the main street, crossing the busy A586 to follow a field path to the river Wyre. The walk then follows the flood embankment of the river with views towards Bowland and across the Fylde. The path leaves the Wyre by the toll bridge and inn at Cartford, before returning to Great Eccleston via field paths and Back Lane.

THE WALK

❶ Starting in the Market Square, walk along the main village street past the Black Bull. Continue along the main street almost to its junction with the A586 and join the main road by turning left and going through an open gateway next to a bus shelter. Take care and go straight across the A road to join the beginning of a hedged lane on the opposite side.

❷ Go down the little lane which leads to a gate and a stile by a waterworks building. Cross the stile and veer right, walking diagonally across the field along a well-used route to the opposite field corner where there is another stile. Climb up the slope to join the embankment of the river Wyre. Note the good views looking eastwards towards the Bowland Fells – including the prominent spurs of Parlick

The village milestone.

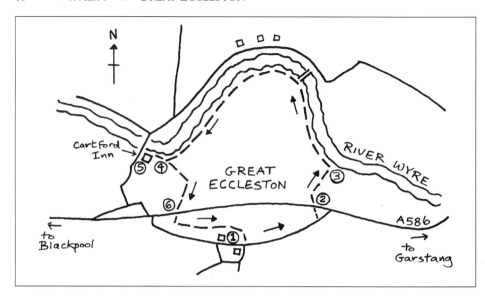

and Fair Snape Fell. The hills rise dramatically from the flood plain of the river Wyre.

❸ Ignore the stile on the embankment leading towards the hills, instead turn left and walk along the embankment in the opposite direction. Continue on this easy to follow embankment for about 1¼ miles to Cartford Bridge. Further stiles are crossed and houses are passed on the far side of the river as it swings around towards the toll bridge.

❹ Just before the bridge a stile is crossed and the path leads through the car park at the rear of the Cartford Inn. You may like to take rest and refreshment here – even though the walk has not been too strenuous. The toll bridge replaced the 'cart ford' crossing upon an old route over the mosses to the villages of Pilling and Cockerham and the inn is believed to have its own resident ghost.

❺ To continue the walk retrace your steps back through the rear car park and look for the ladder stile in a hedge alongside the riverside track. Cross over the stile and head towards the footbridge which can be clearly seen on the far side of the field. Cross the bridge and head to the opposite field corner – you may be able to make out the stile on the far side. Cross this stile and join the hedged track, following it as it swings right and leads back uphill to join the A586.

❻ Take care and go directly across the main road along the footpath which passes cottages. After a very short distance turn left along Back Lane. This lane runs between cottages and the rear of properties fronting the village main street. Follow Back Lane along its entire length until it emerges on the main street alongside a brick-built butcher's shop. Turn right and walk the short distance back to the Market Square.

BARLEY

Length: 2½ miles

Getting there: Barley village is situated on minor roads 2½ miles west of the town of Barrowford, near Nelson. It is best approached either from the A6068 or the A682. If approaching via the M65,

leave at junction 13.

Parking: There is a large car park, picnic area and information centre on the south side of the village which is clearly signposted on arrival. Please

make a donation in the honesty box towards the upkeep of the car park.

Map: OS Landranger 103 Blackburn and Burnley (GR 823404).

Standing at 1,827 feet above sea level, the brooding mass of Pendle Hill is a desolate backdrop to the notorious misdeeds of the infamous Lancashire Witches. In 1612, several witches from the valleys below Pendle Hill were publicly executed at Lancaster after a trial which revealed tales of death curses, murder and sorcery. So the names of Old Demdike, Squintin' Lizzie, Chattox and Alice Nutter passed into local folklore and inspired devilish legends that howl through the gales down the 'Big End' of Pendle Hill to cast shadows over the villages below. John Robinson of

FOOD and DRINK

The stately Pendle Inn draws visitors from far and wide to relax in the comfort of its spacious rooms, with a wide range of meals available in traditional surroundings. Telephone: 01282 614808. Barley also boasts tea rooms and the Barley Mow restaurant. Telephone: 01282 614293.

Barley was a victim of the 17th-century witchcraft, whilst at nearby Newchurch the hags robbed graves at St Mary's church.

Barley itself is an ancient settlement formed in a clearing within the vast medieval hunting reserve known as the Forest of Pendle. It became a focus for cattle rearing and this agricultural scene still predominates today. The valleys around the village have been flooded in this century to create reservoirs to supply neighbouring towns.

This short expedition uncovers some of the delights of Lancashire's 'Witch Country', offering splendid views of Pendle Hill for most of the way. The walk starts at the public car park at Barley and heads south, climbing through fields to arrive at neighbouring Newchurch with its famous 'Witches Galore' shop. The route then follows the Pendle Way recreational path over the moors and through woodland to join the reservoir track alongside the Lower Ogden Reservoir which leads back to the village.

THE WALK

❶ From the main entrance to the car park and picnic area turn right to reach a road junction and then turn left, crossing the road bridge over the stream with Barley village hall on the far side of the road. Walk uphill along the road for 100 yards until you reach the group of cottages known as Bridge End on the left-hand side.

❷ Turn left in front of the cottages and follow the steep stone road uphill between walls. Look back for excellent views of Barley nestling beneath Pendle Hill's 'Big End' (the summit). After 200 yards a wooden stile is joined on the right-hand side of the stone road.

❸ Cross the stile and follow the path uphill, keeping to the wall side. Head for the farmhouse directly ahead and cross the stile in the field corner just to the right of the buildings. Turn right and follow the driveway as it skirts past another farmhouse and stables on your right and then continues slightly uphill to join a public road.

❹ Turn left and follow the narrow road downhill. The road bends round to the

PLACES of INTEREST

An insight into the history, folklore and farming traditions of the Pendle district can be gleaned at **Pendle Heritage Centre** in the nearby town of Barrowford, 2½ miles east of Barley along the minor road which passes through the village of Roughlee. The centre is at Park Hill and is housed in old farm buildings built by the Bannister family. It includes an agricultural museum, walled garden, tea room and shop. Telephone: 01282 695366. For an entirely different experience visit the **Sabden Treacle Mines** which are located in the centre of Sabden village, 3½ miles south-west of Barley along minor lanes. This unique attraction – ideal for kids – has created its own world of curious treacle characters and treacle mines where, of course, you can buy treacle toffee. Telephone: 01282 775279.

The walk visits Newchurch with its famous shop.

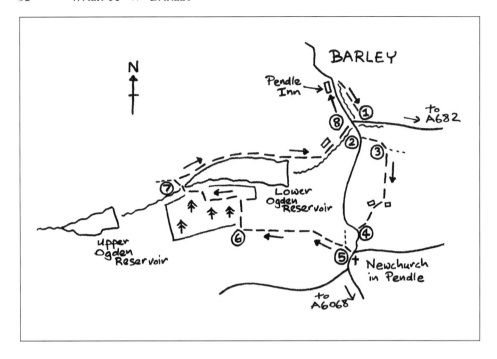

right and enters the interesting little hamlet of Newchurch-in-Pendle, the self-proclaimed capital of 'Witch Country'. You cannot fail to encounter the much photographed cackle of old hags sitting outside the tourist gift shop which offers you a chance to buy all your souvenirs even before the walk is over! Continue past the gift shop only a very short distance and on the same side look out on your right for a path which leads up the steps next to the public toilets. The route is signposted by the distinctive witch way-markers of the Pendle Way.

❺ Climb the steps and as the path forks turn left and cross the stile which leads into a field. Veer right uphill and over the brow a wall comes into view on the far side of the field. Head for the gate opening in the wall

but on reaching it do not go through it, instead turn left and follow the waymarked route, keeping the wall to your right. At the field corner cross a stile and follow the path through the next field with the wall still on your right. Continue in the same direction to the corner of a plantation.

❻ By the corner of the plantation turn right and cross over the stile which leads into another field with the woodland on your left behind a wall. Follow the path downhill with the wall to your left. Just before the bottom corner of the field is reached look out for the stile in the wall and turn left, crossing the stile to enter the woodland. Follow the stone path which winds gradually downhill, eventually zig-zagging down through a series of steep stone steps to emerge at the edge of the plantation at the head of a reservoir. Walk down steps and cross a footbridge over the stream which leads into the Lower Ogden Reservoir to your right. Turn right and follow the waymarkers which lead across another footbridge to a reservoir road beyond a kissing gate.

❼ Turn right and follow the road alongside the Lower Ogden Reservoir. Follow this for ¾ mile, passing by the dam and the ornate Nelson Waterworks (1912). Beyond the Waterworks entrance, cottages are passed on your left and you arrive back at the road alongside Barley village hall.

❽ Turn left but do not return to the car park immediately, instead continue along the road which leads into the village proper with the Pendle Inn on your left. After exploring the village, return to the car park by leaving the roadside on the opposite side to the Pendle Inn, crossing the footbridge which leads alongside the stream to the picnic area and information centre.

HURST GREEN

Length: 8½ miles

Getting there: The village is located 6 miles north of Blackburn and is situated upon the B6243, roughly halfway between Longridge and Clitheroe.

Parking: There is ample parking along the main village street which runs up past the memorial cross opposite the Shireburn Arms towards the Bayley Arms Hotel, the starting point of this walk. The street can be very busy with traffic at weekends.

Map: OS Landranger 103 Blackburn and Burnley (GR 685379).

Since the earliest days of charabanc excursions visitors have been flocking to Hurst Green in search of afternoon teas and wayside inns. The ramblers and cyclists have been coming too, since Victorian days, as the village is an ideal base from which to explore the dense network of paths and lanes criss-crossing this beautifully wooded stretch of the Ribble valley. As well as its setting, Hurst Green's appeal also lies in its history – a history inextricably bound up with the Shireburn family and Stonyhurst College.

Stonyhurst is now one of the most famous Roman Catholic boarding schools in the country and the Jesuit college was established here in 1794. Prior to this it was the home of the manorial lords, the Shireburns – Richard Shireburn having built the Hall in 1592 on his ancestral site. Nicholas Shireburn built the fine almshouses in the village in 1706 and the lords of the manor are even recognised in the name of the Shireburn Arms Hotel.

This expedition goes in search of the river Ribble. Starting by the Bayley Arms Hotel in the village centre, the route follows woodland paths and green lanes to the roadside viewpoint of Crowshaw Quarry. Field paths then lead south to join the Ribble Way and then the river at the Dinckley suspension footbridge. From here the route continues along the river, before turning inland across pastures to reach the architectural gem of Stonyhurst College.

THE WALK

❶ Starting from the Bayley Arms Hotel walk away from the village centre, past the ornate Shireburn Almshouse on your right. Just after the Almshouse, look out for a bridleway leaving the main street on your left – opposite Smithy Lane.

❷ Walk down the track, keeping to the higher level when it forks – do not take the left fork which drops downhill. Continue along the main track and the bridleway drops gradually downhill to follow a woodland stream. Turn left over a footbridge and follow the track as it climbs uphill away from the stream. The track leaves the woodland behind and forms a

FOOD and DRINK

The award-winning Shireburn Arms Hotel records the name of the lords of the manor and is a quality country inn which is happy to welcome walkers. The high standards of the restaurant are also reflected in the exceptionally appetising and filling bar meals. There are daily blackboard specials or why not try 'old favourites' like bangers and mash, liver and onions and shepherd's pie. Dessert specials on the blackboard may include home-made puddings like spotted dick and the intriguing 'Oriental Experience'. Telephone: 01254 826518. Try also the Bayley Arms Hotel, telephone: 01254 826478, and the Eagle and Child, telephone: 01254 826788.

wide green lane between fields. Continue straight ahead to a stone farmhouse called Greengore.

❸ Pass Greengore on your left, cross the stile and follow the track alongside woodland and then through fields. Further stiles are crossed and the track swings right and passes stone farm buildings. The track then becomes a tarmac access road. Follow this slightly uphill, crossing a cattle grid to join a minor road. Turn left along the road, walking uphill for about 200 yards until a small car parking area is reached at Crowshaw Quarry. There is a view indicator here and the viewpoint is excellent, revealing Pendle Hill and the Ribble valley in all its glory.

❹ On the far side of the car park look out for the footpath sign which leads over a cattle grid and down a track to Intack Farm. As the house is passed on your right look out immediately to your left for a stile in the tree hedge. Cross this and veer right, walking diagonally to a stile on the opposite side of the field. Cross this and continue in the same direction in the next field, walking over the brow of a hill and heading downhill to a roadside stile and gate. Cross the stile and join the road. Go straight ahead, walking downhill along the road past Huntingdon Hall. After about ⅓ mile, look out for a signed footpath leaving the road on your left, just in front of a white cottage.

❺ Turn left and follow this farm track to Carlinghurst. The lane drops down to a farmyard and just before the barns a gate and stile are reached on the left leading into a field. Cross the stile and follow the track which ends abruptly in a field by another stile. Swing right here and head for a nearby stile in the field corner to your right. Cross this and walk with the field boundary to your immediate right, heading towards woodland and a farmhouse. The path joins a tarmac lane next to the farmhouse. Turn right along this, crossing a cattle grid, and walk downhill for nearly ½ mile until a main road (between Longridge and Clitheroe) is reached.

❻ Turn left along the road and follow the narrow pavement towards the nearby Punch Bowl pub, which dates from 1793. Unless you are quenching your thirst in the hostelry, turn right along the footpath just before the pub. The path follows a track which swings left around a cottage then climbs uphill. After passing over the brow of a small hill leave the track and turn right to walk diagonally across a field. A waymarker post adjacent to the track points the way. Head for a wooden footbridge on the far side of the large field and cross this, swinging diagonally left from the bridge to cross the next field and reach a wood. Look out for a difficult to find stile at the field boundary with the woodland. Cross the stile and follow the path downhill through the woodland to a footbridge over a stream. The path then leads uphill to another stile which leads onto a farm road.

❼ Turn left and follow the farm road for about ½ mile. Shortly after going through a gateway next to a cottage on your left the path crosses a cattle grid and joins the Ribble Way long-distance path. Follow the

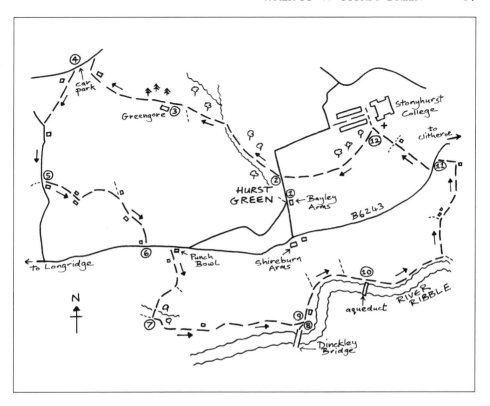

waymarkers and go through the gate to the left of the farm road. The route then follows a field edge down to a footbridge in a field corner below trees. Cross the footbridge and veer right to walk along the field edge with the boundary to your immediate right. Keep close to this boundary and cross further stiles, eventually emerging on a track which runs downhill between conifers. As this track swings left towards farm buildings look out for a stile to your right.

❽ Cross this stile and follow the fenced path between trees for an interesting diversion. The path leads to the Dinckley suspension footbridge, opened in 1951. At last, after several glimpses, there is a proper view of the river Ribble. After resting by the river retrace your steps back to the stile and the track.

❾ Continue along the track, which passes an assortment of farm buildings and leads uphill. When woodland is reached to the right of the track keep a good look out for a stile in the hedge to the right, waymarked with a white arrow. Cross this stile which leads across a field to another stile on the edge of the woodland. A path waymarked with white arrows is now followed which skirts the top edge of woodland. Please note this is a permissive route granted with kind permission of the landowner. After about ⅓ mile the path joins a right of way by a stile. Turn right here and go down the steps through the woodland to a footbridge. After the bridge follow the riverside path to the large aqueduct which crosses the Ribble.

⑩ Cross the stile to the left of the aqueduct and continue alongside the river – crossing more stiles – for a further ¾ mile. Leave the river when a track is met on the left which runs away from the river towards farm buildings. Turn left here and follow the track to the buildings. Just before the barns are reached turn right along a waymarked track across a cattle grid. This leads onto a lane and you continue in the same direction along the lane

which swings left and runs alongside a stream. After passing the entrance to a fine house with an 1898 date stone on the right, go through a gate on the left of the lane. Walk uphill alongside the field boundary and at the top of the hill two more gates lead back onto the Longridge-Clitheroe road.

⑪ Turn left and follow the pavement slightly uphill until a footpath is reached on the opposite side of the road. Take care crossing the road and join this path via a stile. The path follows a hedge side and then continues on a stone track heading straight in the direction of the towers of Stonyhurst College. Beyond farm buildings a lane is joined which leads to the church and the main entrance to the College. Continue straight ahead to take a closer look at the College but the walk continues along the field path which leaves the lane on the left before the church is reached.

⑫ This path skirts woodland on your right and eventually reaches Smithy Lane. Walk down here to rejoin the main village street and turn left to return to the Bayley Arms Hotel.

WHALLEY

Length: 2 miles

Getting there: Situated 5 miles north-east of Blackburn, the village nestles between the A59 and A671 roads from Blackburn and Burnley and is signposted from both routes.	Parking: There are parking places in and around the village, including parking on the main village street at its northern end away from the often busy centre.	Map: OS Landranger 103 Blackburn and Burnley (GR 733362).

Located in the very heart of the county, Whalley can justifiably claim to be one of Lancashire's most famous villages. This is largely due to the historic remains of its abbey which dominate the village. But even before the Abbot Gregory and his 20 Cistercian monks arrived from Cheshire in 1296 to set up the new abbey site, Whalley was already an ancient township and parish of some importance. Its 13th-century church of St Mary – on the site of an earlier church – was the centre of a vast rural parish covering much of the Ribble valley.

This short walk is essential for anyone wanting to appreciate the superb natural setting of Whalley, nestling in a lush valley against a backdrop of hills. The Nab, on the south side of the village, is Whalley's own 'Matterhorn' and this walk climbs the Nab along well-trodden paths to gain an excellent view of the ancient township below. Starting in the village centre by the pubs, the walk passes the entrance to the abbey and the gatehouse before crossing the river Calder and going under the dominating railway viaduct from where the walk climbs uphill to Whalley Old Road and the steep slopes of the Nab. From excellent viewpoints the route descends from Nab Wood to the road bridge over the Calder to continue along King Street.

THE WALK

❶   By the four pubs in the centre of the village turn down Church Lane, which begins alongside the De Lacey Arms and is signposted to the church of St Mary and Whalley Abbey. Keep to the lane as it winds past the church, a school and the entrance to the abbey and then runs under the Gate Tower, which dates from 1318. After a very short distance pass under the

tall brick railway viaduct which carries the Blackburn-Clitheroe railway. The viaduct was built across the low-lying Calder valley in the late 1840s and the 48 arched brick structure is a remarkable example of Victorian engineering.

❷   Turn left immediately and follow the tarmac footpath which runs parallel to the viaduct and crosses Old Saul's Bridge over the river Calder. A plaque on the bridge explains the history of this crossing and its association with a local mill owner, Solomon Longworth. The path soon joins a road.

❸   At the road turn left and go back under the viaduct, then turn immediately right up a residential avenue (Walmsley Brow). At the top of the avenue, pass a terraced row and climb the steps to join the road alongside the Ebenezer Baptist chapel. Cross the road and climb the step

Entrance to the 14th-century abbey near the start of the walk.

stile to follow the continuation of the footpath which runs uphill between fields, reaching Whalley Old Road at a stone stile near to cottages.

❹ Turn right and follow the road for about 260 yards until a signed footpath is reached on the left-hand side of the road at a gap in the wall. This is immediately after passing the property called Casamonte. Leave the road here and climb the steep slope on the left-hand side of a wooded ravine. Near the top of the ravine cross a stile and continue in the same direction through trees to cross another stile that leads onto a narrow lane.

❺ Turn left and walk down the lane, passing a footpath sign on your left from where there are excellent views looking towards the railway viaduct and across the Calder valley. Ignore this footpath though, but very shortly on the right-hand side of the lane another footpath is reached which points up the drive of the property called Wood Nook.

❻ Go up the driveway, passing the cottage on your left, and enter a field via a stile. The path now swings around the hillside along the line of a stone wall embankment. The panoramic view reveals Whalley in all its glory – pick out the abbey and the main village street against the dramatic backdrop of the outlying Bowland hills. At the end of the stone wall veer right across the field to reach the

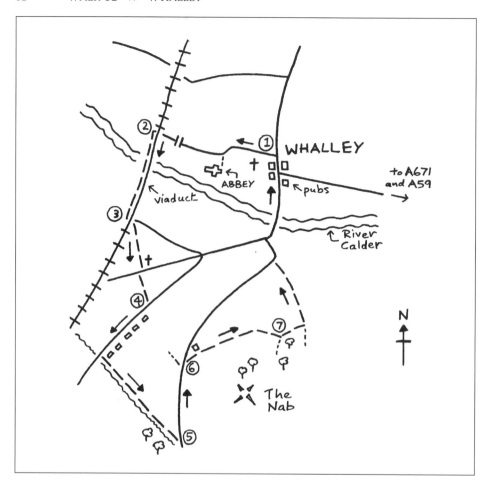

edge of a small wood. On reaching the trees, turn left alongside a fence and drop down to join the stone track below via a stile to the right of a cattle grid.

❼ Turn right and follow the track below trees as it swings right and is joined on the left by a waymarked bridleway alongside a wall. Leave the track here, turning sharp left and proceeding downhill, following a sunken path with the wall on your right. The path descends steeply to rejoin the lane (Moor Lane). Continue downhill and when the lane meets a main road by the bridge, turn right and cross the bridge over the river Calder. Continue straight ahead along King Street and the numerous shops and pubs quickly come into view.

WREA GREEN

Length: 4½ miles

Getting there: The village is situated on the B5259, 2 miles west of Kirkham. Wrea Green is signposted from the A583 on the west side of Kirkham which is halfway between Preston and Blackpool.

Parking: There is ample space for parking around the large village green.

Map: OS Landranger 102 Preston and Blackpool (GR 316396).

Wrea Green's most distinctive feature also gives the village its name – for the broad village green is the largest in Lancashire. Around it are arranged picture postcard houses and little appears to have changed – apart from the flash cars – since the Victorian days when assorted traders and pedlars would stop off in the village and move from cottage to cottage around the green selling their wares. Ducks and geese flapped around the green even before the Romans marched across the Ribble and passed through nearby Kirkham. They can still be found relaxing in the pond which was created by the removal of clay for house building.

for the Fylde resorts, but it has not gone unnoticed. Many visitors stop off here to break their journey to Blackpool and on summer weekends the rusticity of the village green is obscured by traffic congestion.

The walk starts from the Grapes pub which overlooks the village green and it is a pleasant stroll through pastures south of the village, via Bryning and then Ribby, with excellent views south across the Ribble estuary.

The village quietly watches over the southern fringes of the Fylde coast and south from here the good agricultural land gradually falls away to the low-lying Ribble Marshes. Wrea Green is a relative haven of peace and quiet between busy A roads filled with holiday traffic on route

THE WALK

❶ From the Grapes cross the village green and head for its opposite corner – to the road signed 'Moss Lane East'. Follow this lane along the pavement past houses with pretty gardens but when the houses end cross over to the left-hand side of the

View of the village pub from across the green.

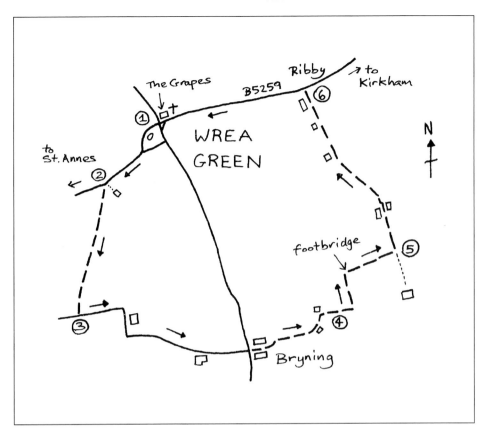

road and join a hedged lane signed as a public footpath.

❷ Walk down the lane which soon ends at a stile leading into a field. Cross the stile and continue in the same direction along the field edge, pass under pylons and gradually climb uphill to reach another stile alongside a lane.

❸ Turn left and follow the lane which winds past farmhouses including Bryning Hall. After about ½ mile the lane reaches a T-junction with another road. Take care and cross this road to follow, almost

directly opposite, a narrow farm lane running alongside the Wrea Green Equitation Centre. The lane winds past several farmhouses before it ends at a stile.

❹ Cross the stile and follow a deeply rutted track. After a very short distance leave the track via a small wooden gate which leads into a field. Climb uphill across the field, firstly along the fence line and then – when the fence changes direction – head directly under the pylons towards a stile in a hedge corner. Wrea Green's church spire can be spotted from here and there are views south towards the uphill. Cross the stile into the adjoining field now with the hedge to your left. Shortly, a stile with a waymarker post is reached alongside a farm lane.

❺ Turn left along the farm lane and walk uphill past Dale Farm and Windrush Farm. The lane is now followed for about ½ mile; it bends left and after passing the red brick buildings of Brown's Farm it joins the main road into the village.

Ribble estuary. Cross the stile and walk along the hedge side to cross a small footbridge. Walk alongside the hedge to your right in a large field which slopes steeply

❻ Turn left along this road, the B5259, and follow the pavement back into the village centre, passing rows of attractive gardened terraces and thatched cottages.

WORSTHORNE

Length: 3 ¾ miles

Getting there: The village is situated high on the moors 2½ miles directly east of Burnley. From Burnley town centre follow the road uphill from Turf Moor (Burnley FC) and sign-posts point left to Worsthorne.

Parking: There are spaces in and around the village centre, including the village end of Gorple Road which begins on

the north side of the church of St John the Evangelist.

Map: OS Landranger 103 Blackburn and Burnley (GR 875325).

Lancashire literally ends at Worsthorne. This forgotten moorland community hides itself away on a shelf of the Pennines overlooking Burnley, but head directly east from the village and there is nothing but bleak hills for several miles before the scattered farmsteads of Hebden Bridge are reached in Yorkshire. The old packhorse road over the moors from Worsthorne can still be followed, a reminder of those 18th century days when the traditional wool trades depended on a sturdy mule and a good stone road to link the village communities of the Lancashire and Yorkshire textile districts. The road from Worsthorne climbed over to the Hebden

FOOD and DRINK

The large Tetley's house on Extwistle Road is the Crooked Billet which is a popular port of call for passing motorists lured by its wide selection of bar meals served in such handsome surroundings. Look out for the blackboard specials here. Telephone: 01282 429040. On the opposite side of the village green try the late-Victorian Bay Horse. Telephone: 01282 437494.

valley via the far-reaching farming settlement of Gorple – which is now just scattered remains of buildings and stone walls.

The walk starts at Worsthorne's village green and follows a stretch of the old packhorse road high onto the moors before dropping down to follow the little valley of the Hurst Brook which leads into Hurstwood Reservoir. A reservoir road takes you into the secretive hamlet of Hurstwood with its 16th-century cottages and then a well-used field path between the hamlet and Worsthorne's church leads back into the centre of the village.

THE WALK

❶ From the village green facing the church of St John the Evangelist join Gorple Road which begins on the left-hand side of the church. Follow this lane uphill as it climbs beyond cottages to become a wide stone bridle road, following a straight course up towards the high Pennine moors. From the village, the road is followed for 1 mile before it reaches a gate on the brow of a hill. Note the fine views back to industrial East Lancashire.

❷ After the gate the road veers slightly left and runs around the hillside. The view

to the right reveals the steep secluded valley of Hurstwood Brook which flows down into the reservoir far below. Walk for about ⅓ mile from the gate on the hillside but then leave the old road by joining a distinct path to your right coming up from the valley below – the path is indicated by a waymarker post. The old road continues its lonely journey eastwards over the Pennines into Yorkshire – the county boundary is only a mile away at this point.

❸ Turn sharp right and follow the path down the valley in the direction of Hurstwood Reservoir below. The path crosses the brook and then follows it closely along its left-hand side. When the stream reaches the reservoir inlet do not cross the nearby footbridge but continue along the main track with the reservoir on your immediate right. After walking the length of the reservoir you reach a gateway to the left of the dam.

PLACES of INTEREST

Historic old halls are a surprising feature of several East Lancashire textile towns and two fine examples can be found within 20 minutes drive of Worsthorne. **Towneley Hall** is Burnley's showpiece and is just 1½ miles south of the town centre along the A646. Set in extensive parkland, the originally medieval Hall was the mansion of the Towneleys, the most important family in the district. It now houses the town museum and art gallery as well as a craft centre and includes some of the most finely furnished rooms in the whole county. Telephone: 01282 24213. On the outskirts of Padiham, 2 miles to the west of Burnley along the A671, is the late Elizabethan country house of **Gawthorpe Hall** which contains important collections of portraits, lace and embroidery. Telephone: 01282 778511.

Gorple Road leading to the moors.

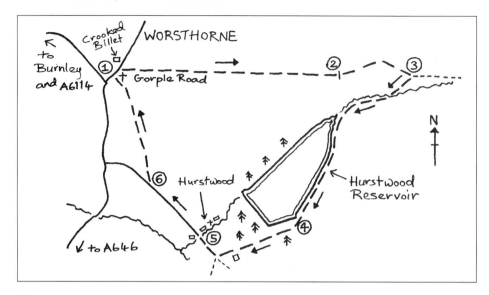

❹ Go through the gateway which crosses over a drain and follow the reservoir road slightly downhill through a small woodland plantation. Pass a pumping station on the left then cross a stile and go through a gate to emerge in a Water Authority picnic area and car park. Follow the main track which swings right and crosses a stone bridge over the brook to arrive at the secluded hamlet of Hurstwood.

❺ Take time to explore the hamlet where time almost appears to have stood still since Tudor days. Interesting properties include the gabled Hurstwood Hall, dating from 1579 and built by the Towneley family, together with the 16th-century cottage of the Spenser family – where the great Elizabethan poet Edmund Spenser spent part of his youth. Note also Hurst-

wood's sober chapel with its 'Life Gate'. From the red phone box by the bridge, the walk continues by turning left and then right along the road out of the hamlet. The road climbs uphill past 'suburban' type houses until a footpath signpost is reached on the right-hand side.

❻ Cross the stile and follow this path which is signposted for 'Worsthorne ½ mile'. Keep to the wall side and cross further stiles to follow the well-used field path which heads directly towards Worsthorne's prominent church tower. The path reaches a kissing gate adjacent to the rear of houses and then becomes a paved route which continues to the south side of the church of St John the Evangelist. Turn left to walk around the front of the sombre-looking church and reach the village green.

HOGHTON

Length: 4 miles

Getting there: The village is situated on the A675, 6 miles east of Preston and 5 miles west of Blackburn. Access to the village can also be gained from junction 3 of the M65 which is just to the south. The village is also easily located from all directions by following the brown tourist signposts for Hoghton Tower.

Parking: Along the roadside at the village end of Chapel Lane, which is the starting point of this walk. There is also limited parking on the roadside outside the Boar's Head pub.

Map: OS Landranger 103 Blackburn and Burnley (GR 613268).

James I passed through this rolling countryside in 1617 and was bountifully entertained for three days as a guest at Hoghton Tower. Sir Richard Hoghton proved an excellent host for it was here, upon the long table in the Elizabethan banqueting hall, that the King used his sword to knight a most delicious loin of beef – and so the 'sir loin' was born.

The present fortified mansion was built by Thomas Hoghton in the 1560s though the tower was destroyed during a Civil War skirmish in the 1640s. Parliamentary troops were billeted in the village and laid siege to the Tower as the Hoghtons were Royalist sympathisers. The family's 19th-century legacy to the neighbouring villagers included restoring the parish church of Holy Trinity and erecting a village school.

The walk starts along Chapel Lane, close to the Boar's Head pub, and explores the hilly countryside of the river Darwen valley along field and woodland paths. The circuit is punctuated by three surprising highlights: a giant railway viaduct over the deep valley gorge, a stretch on the towpath of the Leeds and Liverpool Canal, and a close view of Hoghton Tower itself as the final stage of the walk enters the grounds of the historic estate.

THE WALK

❶ Start the walk by following Chapel Lane which leaves the main A675 road just south of the Boar's Head. Parliamentary troops were barracked at cottages on the lane during the time of the English Civil War. Walk along the pavement past all the houses until a footpath is reached

on the right-hand side of the lane which can be seen leading uphill through a field.

❷ Cross the stile and join the path, keeping to the left-hand side of the field boundary. At the top end of the field a door in a high wall is reached; turn left here and walk alongside the wall, crossing another stile which leads into woodland. Where the wall starts to veer to the right, leave it and follow the sunken track which leads directly ahead. Shortly, the path emerges at white gates alongside the railway line itself.

❸ This railway line runs between Preston and Blackburn and is in regular use – so take great care crossing it – stop, look, listen and beware of trains! Turn right immediately after crossing the tracks and follow the bridleway which runs close by the railway before dropping downhill to join the end of a lane alongside a group of cottages.

Narrowboats on the Leeds and Liverpool canal.

❹ Turn right onto the lane and follow the path running above the stone houses and immediately below the railway embankment. Very shortly a high railway viaduct is reached which traverses the deep gorge of the river Darwen. Continue under the viaduct and follow the riverside path. The river Darwen rises in the moors and flows through Blackburn before flowing northwards to join the Ribble. After ½ mile the wooded gorge opens out to reach a ladder stile in the corner of a large field.

❺ Cross the ladder stile and leave the river behind, instead swinging right to climb the steep stone track which leads uphill between trees. Another stile is soon crossed and the path leads to a wooden kissing gate on the far side of a small field.

Beyond the gate bear left and follow the meandering farm track between hedges for ¼ mile until it reaches the main A6061 road.

❻ Take care and cross the A6061, then turn left and follow the pavement for 80 yards until a footpath is reached on the right. Follow this path downhill between hedges, passing a field with a crop of radio masts! The path soon swings sharp right and leads onto the towpath of the Leeds and Liverpool Canal.

❼ Turn right onto the towpath and head under the nearby road bridge. Shortly after passing under the road look out for a large stile in the hedge to the right. Leave the towpath here and cross further stiles

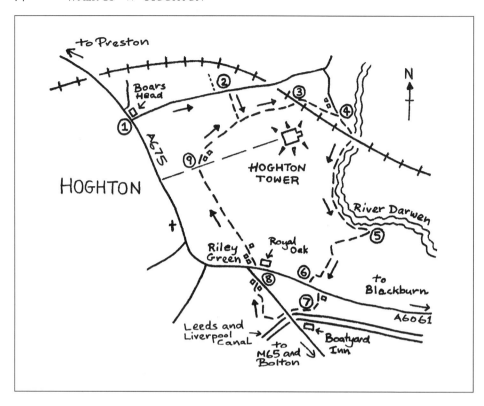

through fields before swinging right between farm buildings to reach the main road. Turn left and follow the A675 road to the junction at Riley Green.

❽ Head for the Royal Oak on the far side of the road and on the nearside of the hostelry join the footpath which begins as a lane alongside cottages. Head directly for the ladder stile at the end of the lane and cross it to enter fields. The route now runs directly uphill for ¼ mile, crossing several ladder stiles before entering the woodland of Hoghton Tower which has itself come

into view. After passing through the band of woodland the path drops downhill to join the main driveway.

❾ The private drive is certainly an impressive approach to the hilltop mansion of the Hoghton family, but continue beyond the drive along the gravel track past stone cottages. Cross a stile and keep to the wall side until another stile is crossed and you meet the path followed at the start of this walk. Turn left and walk downhill to rejoin Chapel Lane.

WHEELTON

Length: 6 miles

Getting there: Wheelton is situated alongside the A674 Chorley-Blackburn road and is 3 miles from Chorley. It is signposted from the A674 which bypasses the village.

Parking: There is ample parking in Wheelton, particularly along the section of the main street which runs from the Red Cat pub down to the Red Lion in the village centre.

Maps: OS Landranger 102 Preston and Blackpool and 109 Manchester (GR 600212).

Wheelton, translating as the 'place on a circular hill', can trace its roots back at least to the 12th century but is now very much a forgotten village. The nearby Leeds and Liverpool Canal and the glory days of cotton spinning brought a golden age to Wheelton in the 19th century but the village mill has gone and even the main Chorley to Blackburn road has bypassed the village since the 1960s.

But the disappearance of passing traffic is a blessing and Wheelton's industrial legacy can still be seen in the terraced rows of workers' cottages which continue to generate a community atmosphere in the village. Wheelton is a classic example of a Victorian mill village, one of several which scatter the moors between Chorley, Blackburn and Bolton.

The walk starts at the Red Lion in the centre of the village and follows lanes and tracks beyond Blackburn Road to uncover some of the delights of this western edge of the West Pennine Moors. A walk along reservoirs leads to beckside cottages in the pretty hamlet of White Coppice and from here a path along the waterway known as the Goit leads to Brinscall Hall. Dramatic moorland views are enjoyed near the end of this walk before the route returns to Wheelton along the road from Brinscall village.

THE WALK

❶ Start on the main village street between the Red Lion and the war memorial. Facing the pub, turn right and walk uphill past the police station to join the busy A674 (Chorley-Blackburn) road. Take great care and cross this to continue the walk up Chapel Lane which is on the

opposite side. Follow the pavement up the hill for just over ¼ mile until the imposing church of St Barnabas is reached. After passing the car park at the rear of the church a lane to the right is reached, which is signed as a footpath.

❷ Turn right and walk down the lane, taking the right fork when the lane divides at the entrance to the property called Eagle Tower. The lane soon ends at the rear of another property on your right but continue straight ahead, crossing a stile, and follow the field edge to another stile. Keep close to the line of trees along a stream bed to your right. The trees swing left and a surprising railway bridge will be seen ahead. Go under the bridge and continue along the distinct grass track alongside a wall until a lane is reached.

The delightful hamlet of White Coppice.

❸ At the lane continue straight ahead across the junction to join the lane signposted to Anglezarke. Follow this past new houses on your right until a footpath signpost is reached on the left-hand side of the lane.

❹ Turn left along this path which quickly leads to the corner of a fishing reservoir. By the corner of the reservoir climb the steep bank which leads to an adjoining reservoir at the back of a car park. Join the distinct track which leads along the right bank of this reservoir. Pass this and cross a stile to continue along the right bank of a third reservoir which ends at a footbridge. Follow the grass path which crosses another footbridge and leads out to a lane overlooked by picturesque cottages.

❺ The unspoilt hamlet of White Coppice has been reached. Turn right and follow the lane which runs straight ahead past the white painted Brookside Cottages with lovely gardens that run down to the stream. The name of the hamlet is believed to have derived from the fact that all the cottages were painted white. The lane becomes a rough track shortly after passing the cottages, but continue straight ahead past the nursery (a green shed) and further reservoirs on your left to arrive at White Coppice's cricket ground – famous for its pretty moorland setting.

❻ Do not take the track which leads to the pavilion but turn left around the cricket pitch, following the track which leads to three pretty white cottages which

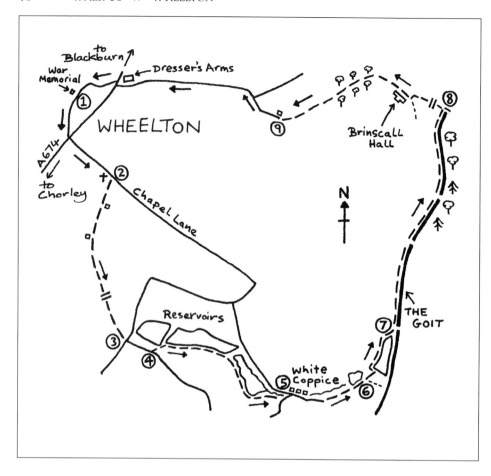

have a grandstand view of the local cricket. After the last cottage turn left and go through the gap which leads to a narrow path between the reservoir bank and the garden hedge. Go through the field gate and turn right to follow a well used permissive route along the reservoir edge. Go through the next field gate and follow the path which swings right to meet a bridge over a waterway known as the Goit. This is an artificial waterway created to link reservoirs to the north and south.

❼ Do not cross the bridge but continue along the left-hand bank of the waterway, following a clear path beneath trees. This path is now followed – with the Goit to your right – for 1 mile and is a permissive route granted with kind permission of the landowner. Two further bridges are passed on the right alongside the path but only leave the Goit when the path alongside it ends by a third bridge, on the far side of which is a gate. Beyond this bridge the Goit suddenly disappears to run underground.

❽ Turn left here and cross a lane to continue beneath a bridge of the disused railway crossed under earlier in the walk. The track now leads uphill and you turn left at the top and then right to walk past the rear of Brinscall Hall which dates from 1876. Continue along the track which leads through two gates and veers left to climb slightly uphill between an avenue of trees. There are commanding views of the West Pennine Moors from here. After the trees end continue along the grass track to the brow of a hill. When the track peters out swing right towards cottages which can be seen nearby. Cross the stile between the cottages to join a little lane.

❾ Follow this and it soon meets a road called Briar's Brow. Turn left – be aware of possible traffic at the bend in the road – and follow it downhill. Take care as there is no pavement at first and the route is used by traffic heading to and from Brinscall village. Eventually the pavement is reached on the right-hand side; continue downhill until busy Blackburn Road is reached alongside the popular Dresser's Arms. Cross the main road with care and continue opposite down Victoria Street. The street is lined with interesting cottages and leads back down to the Red Lion at the bottom of the hill.

BELMONT
Length: 3¾ miles

Getting there: The village is situated on the A675, 6 miles north of Bolton and 14 miles south of Preston. If approaching on the M61 leave at junction 6 and head for Horwich.

Parking: Along the main village street or on the roadside by the 'Blue Lagoon' which is just behind St Peter's church.

Map: OS Landranger 109 Manchester (GR 675158).

There were only a few scattered farmhouses hereabouts until the Industrial Revolution swept through South Lancashire and gave birth to the mill village of Belmont. The textile trade created a burgeoning rural community which was inextricably linked with the fortunes of the cloth bleaching and dyeing works, established just a stone's throw from the Black Dog inn.

The physical legacy of Belmont's past industrial boom can still be seen today in the sturdy rows of brick terraces, the reservoirs and lodges (providing water power to the mills) and the Victorian bleach and dye works itself, founded by entrepreneur

Edward Deakin. Almost opposite the Black Dog is St Peter's church.

The spire of St Peter's and the tall chimney of the bleach works are distinctive landmarks on view for much of the walk. Starting from the Black Dog, this circuit combines moorland and valley paths which reveal the majestic rural setting of Belmont – 'beautiful hill'. There are breathtaking views of the West Pennines, an intimate stroll through the secluded valley of Longworth Clough and a look at the rural industry which still beats at the heart of modern day Belmont.

The Walk

❶ From the Black Dog walk up the main village street past the post office. Terraced rows predominate and were built for workers in the 19th century. Beyond the houses leave the right-hand side of the road where it bends, by taking a short path which leads down to Belmont Reservoir. This is now the base of Bolton Sailing Club, but it was created in 1827 to provide water for Belmont's fledgling industries.

❷ Turn right and follow the road along the edge of the reservoir. Beyond the water

the road veers right and shortly a way-marked stile is reached on the left-hand side alongside a small wood. Cross the stile and follow the waymarked route uphill across fields. The path skirts a forest plantation and eventually reaches a distinctive memorial signpost (number 235) erected by the Peak and Northern Footpaths Preservation Society.

❸ From the Peak and Northern signpost take a right turn and follow the farm track which runs alongside a large forest plantation. The track winds downhill to a gate by the side of a road. Cross over and walk directly ahead along the adjoining minor road which climbs uphill to another road junction. At this T-junction cross over and climb over the wall stile directly opposite which leads into Longworth Clough Nature Reserve. Note the fine view of Belmont's church spire from here.

❹ Drop steeply down into the wooded valley and cross the fast-flowing stream over a footbridge. Turn right immediately

View towards the church at Belmont.

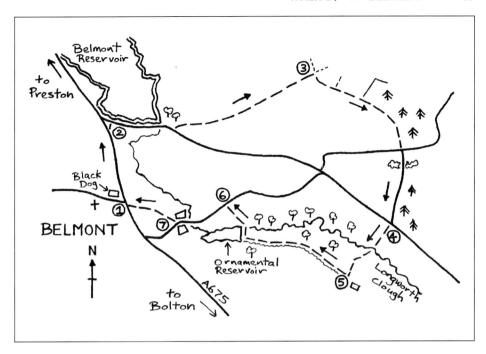

on the far side of the stream and climb the steep slope out of the valley to a stile in a field corner above the woodland. Cross the stile and veer slightly to the right of the nearby house until a path is joined on the nearside bank of a drainage channel just before the house is reached.

❺ Walk alongside the channel for nearly ½ mile, heading in the direction of Belmont church. Eventually an artificial lake, known locally as the Ornamental Reservoir, is reached. Cross the reservoir bank and footbridge and climb uphill to a metal field gate by the road.

❻ Turn left and follow the road downhill until the works of the Belmont Bleaching and Dyeing Company are reached. The road passes between the sheds which belch out steam and provide a lingering reminder of Belmont's industrial heyday. Edward Deakin bought the mill buildings here about 1870 and his enterprise exported finished cotton goods to Africa and China. Many moorland watercourses converge here as the processes required constant supplies of pure water.

❼ Turn right immediately beyond the works and climb the steep path (by the bollards) which leads up to the village along the terraced row known as Maria Square. This neat row is the oldest terraced street in the village, dating from 1804. Maria Square quickly leads back to the main street and the Black Dog. Note the interesting horse trough on the corner by the pub car park, erected in 1897 to celebrate Queen Victoria's Diamond Jubilee.

TURTON
Length: 7½ miles

Getting there: Turton is 4½ miles north of Bolton and is reached by following the B6391 from Bromley Cross train station. North of Turton Tower the road bends right but con- tinue straight ahead uphill along the road signed as the High Street; this leads to Chapeltown.

Parking: Some parking is avail- able on the roadside in the High Street.

Map: OS Landranger 109 Manchester (GR 734158).

'Turton' has its roots in Old Norse language and was the original name of the hilltop community now known as Chapel- town which adopted the new name when it acquired a church.

At the heart of the valley of the Brad- shaw Brook was Turton Tower, originally built for the lord of the manor in the 15th century. The Tower's residents witnessed many changes to the district in the 18th and 19th centuries as tall mill chimneys appeared upon stream banks. Quite appro- priately, in 1835, it passed into the hands of a cotton manufacturer, James Kay.

Water and woodlands dominate this walk which starts at the Chethams Arms

FOOD and DRINK

The stone built Chethams Arms fits neatly between the old cottages lining the High Street and takes its name from Humphrey Chetham, the great Manchester merchant who bought Turton Tower in 1628. The cosy village pub remains at the heart of the close-knit community but is most welcoming to visitors. It is known for its classic steaks but look out for the blackboard on the wall outside that highlights daily specials such as a rack of ribs. Telephone: 01204 852279. The Strawbury Duck at Entwistle, half way round the walk is also worth a visit. Telephone: 01204 852013.

along the main street of stone cottages in Chapeltown. The route follows a circuit around the valley of Bradshaw Brook which was transformed to create three reservoirs to supply water to the burgeoning urban population of nearby Bolton. Along the way there are unexpected delights – an isolated inn famous for its real ale and a castellated railway bridge upon the approach to Turton Tower.

THE WALK

❶ From the Chethams Arms walk along the High Street in the direction away from the parish church of St Anne with its prominent spire. Follow the road out of the village for nearly ¼ mile until Embankment Road is reached on the right-hand side. Turn down this road, which leads through a gate down to the corner of the dam of Wayoh Reservoir. Continue across the high dam to reach a track on the far side of the reservoir.

❷ Turn left and follow the track skirting the right-hand edge of the reservoir. Ahead can be seen the viaduct of the Bolton-Blackburn railway. After crossing a lane continue along the track all the way to the upper end of Wayoh Reservoir until a footbridge is reached. Cross this and a second footbridge to reach a path junction. Follow the path which veers slightly left and climbs up a hill between trees – it is waymarked as the 'Warper's Trail'. The path emerges at a field; cross this and go through the gate to join a lane.

❸ Turn right and follow the lane which turns sharp left over a railway bridge. Ahead of you is the Strawbury Duck Inn, a popular pub that has put the tiny hamlet of Entwistle on the map. Continue along the signed footpath skirting around the front of the pub; this follows a private road past a terrace of railway houses. Follow the road downhill and cross the dam of the Turton and Entwistle Reservoir which stretches northwards.

PLACES of INTEREST

Turton Tower is passed en route. This originally 15th-century pele tower was the home of many distinguished families such as the Orrells, Chethams and Kays. It has been finely restored and includes a museum. Telephone: 01204 852203. Less than a mile down the road to Bromley Cross from Turton, follow the signs that lead to the **Last Drop Village**, a collection of antique and gift shops on an old street surrounding a popular hotel. Here you can photograph yourself in the village stocks. Telephone: 01204 591131. Continue even further down the road towards Bolton to arrive at the town's most famous historic property, **Hall i' th' Wood**, a Tudor manor house – now a museum – which was the former home of the inventor of the spinning mule, Samuel Crompton. Telephone: 01204 301159.

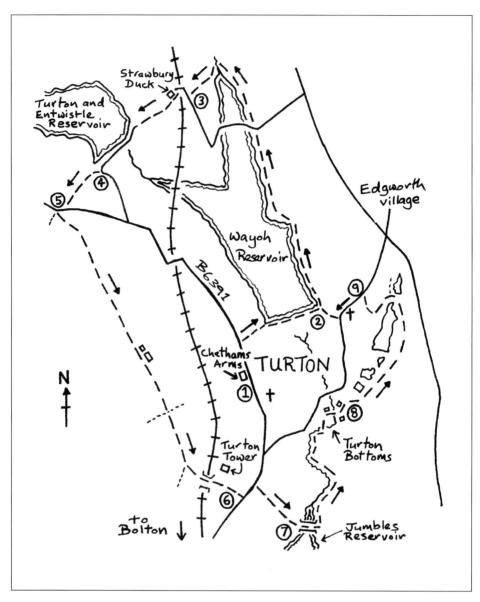

❹ On the far side pass the car park and where the road bends sharp left go directly ahead up a flight of steps cut into the embankment overlooking the road. Turn right to reach a higher level car park. From here follow the grass track to your left way-marked as the 'Warper's Trail'. The track climbs uphill and enters a field beyond a stile. Follow the waymarks, continuing uphill beyond the reservoir access road and very shortly another road is reached by a stile.

❺ Turn right and walk along this road for about 80 yards until two footpaths join it on the left-hand side. Follow the path signed as the private road leading to Clough House Farm. The farm track runs downhill providing fine views across the valley of Bradshaw Brook towards Turton and Edgworth. Keep to the track for about 1¼ miles until it forks after passing through a kissing gate. Follow the left fork which leads downhill alongside a stream and shortly the railway is crossed via an ornate castellated bridge. Continue past the restored water wheel of Black Rock Mill which powered Turton's 19th-century cotton industry and Turton Tower quickly comes into view. Continue along the driveway to reach a road.

❻ Turn left and follow the road downhill for about 250 yards before crossing carefully to join a footpath on the right-hand side of the road. This leads uphill along a field edge, then crosses a stile and runs downhill through trees to reach a wide bridge over the inlet to Jumbles Reservoir – the third reservoir encountered on this walk.

❼ Cross the bridge and on the far side turn immediately left to walk upstream along a riverside path. Follow this path for about ½ mile until you reach cottages. Cross the brook and follow a little cobbled lane uphill which soon bends sharp right to cross the brook again. As the cobbled lane begins to wind left to join the road take a right fork past a row of cottages and then beyond them there is a junction of paths.

❽ Take the path veering left which climbs diagonally up a hillside and overlooks little reservoirs. Follow this waymarked route above the reservoirs until it drops to a footbridge. Cross this and turn left to climb up the opposite side of the valley, turning right to join a stone lane. Follow this lane between cottages to the road in Edgworth village.

❾ Turn left and follow the pavement downhill past the Methodist church until the Black Bull Hotel is reached on the opposite side of the road. Join the signed public footpath which runs alongside the pub and this quickly leads back down to the reservoir dam. From here retrace your steps back to the Chethams Arms at Chapeltown.

RUFFORD

Length: 4 miles

Getting there: The village is situated on the A59 Liverpool-Preston road and is 2½ miles north of Burscough Bridge.

Parking: The A59 is a busy trunk road unsuitable for parking. But to the east of the road there are a limited number of spaces along Liverpool Road by the village stores and also along Church Road which is just off the B5246 leading eastwards out of the village.

Map: OS Landranger 108 Liverpool (GR 461156).

The Rufford district is linked with the Hesketh family who acquired their estate at Rufford as early as the 13th century in what was then a boggy marsh at the edge of a vast inland lake known as Martin Mere. Hereabouts was the 'rough ford' over a channel draining into the nearby river Douglas. Robert Hesketh built what is now Rufford Old Hall in the 1530s on the site of an earlier 15th century family residence. When Martin Mere was largely drained in the 19th century the estate village around the Hall developed into a productive farming community.

Rufford Old Hall, owned by the National Trust since 1936, still dominates

FOOD and DRINK

The only pub in the village centre is the Hesketh Arms, not a surprising name bearing in mind the village developed on the estate of the Hesketh family. The pub was formerly a coaching inn on the Liverpool-Preston highway and had stables for horses, now superseded by a large car park. As an old coaching inn, the provision of good food for weary travellers has a long tradition here and a wide range of reasonably priced meals are provided together with Greenalls Bitter. Telephone: 01704 821716.

the village and the Hesketh name is prominently recorded in the wayside pub on the main Liverpool-Preston road. Canal trade also came to the village in 1781 when the Rufford branch of the Leeds and Liverpool Canal opened, providing a transport corridor for coal from the south to the north of the county.

The walk follows lanes out of the village to explore the woodland and lakes of the nationally important Mere Sands Wood Nature Reserve. From here green lanes between cultivated fields are followed which offer fine views across the flat West Lancashire plain. The final leg of the walk follows the grassy towpath of the tranquil Rufford Canal, with glimpses of the black and white timbers of the historic Rufford Old Hall.

THE WALK

❶ From the village post office on Liverpool Road, take care and cross the busy A59 to reach the Hesketh Arms on the opposite side of the road. Join the pavement on Holmeswood Road, which is signed alongside the pub, and walk along this past the school until Brick Kiln Lane

is reached – the second turning on the left – opposite Hesketh Lodge. Walk down Brick Kiln Lane past houses until two footpath signposts are reached on either side of the lane alongside a stream.

❷ Cross the stream and turn right to follow the narrow footpath which runs along its left-hand side. After a short distance the path emerges on a residential road, cross this and follow the continuation of the path which now runs along the right-hand side of the stream, through gateway leading to Rufford Cricket Club. Follow the field edge and pass through a kissing gate to enter Mere Sands Wood Nature Reserve. The reserve is managed by the Lancashire Wildlife Trust and is a haven for wildlife including red squirrels.

❸ By the information board at the entrance to the reserve, turn right and follow the main path which skirts around

PLACES of INTEREST

Rufford Old Hall is located on the north side of the village between the A59 and the Rufford Canal. The National Trust property details the history of the Hesketh home which includes the timber Great Hall, a gift shop, a tea room and extensive gardens and woodland. Telephone: 01704 821254. **Mere Sands Wood Nature Reserve**, created on ponds formed by sand extraction, is entered during the walk. Telephone: 01704 821809. But to explore the wildlife of the remaining marshlands of West Lancashire in more detail then visit **Martin Mere**, a large reserve of the Wildfowl and Wetlands Trust just 2½ miles south-west of Rufford off the road between Burscough Bridge and Holmeswood. Take your binoculars and tick off the many different species to be found here which include migrating swans and geese. Telephone: 01704 895181.

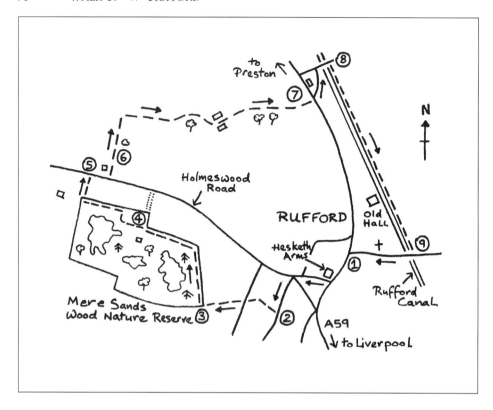

the edge of the woodland. Time may be taken to explore the hides and viewing platforms which are reached to the left of the main path, but the walk then continues along the woodland edge, eventually reaching the reserve's car park and visitor centre.

❹ Continue the walk by following the path which leads off from the edge of the car park (signed as the 'brown route') through woodland. By a hide the path turns sharp right and then left when it reaches the edge of the wood. Keep to the main path along the woodland fringe and when the path forks at an information board take the right fork to reach a wooden footbridge. Cross this and go directly across the field to a hedge gap alongside a road.

❺ Take care and cross this road to join the pavement and turn right. After a short distance an access road is reached on the left alongside a cottage called The Warren. Turn left and follow the access road which reaches a field and becomes a distinct grass track between fields.

❻ Follow the grass track until it joins another one beyond a small pond and turn right to head towards woodland. The green lane joins a stone track; follow this in the same direction, entering the woodland and continuing on the track as it

Mere Sands Wood Nature Reserve.

passes between semi-derelict farm buildings. The track then runs gradually downhill to join the A59 alongside cottages. On clear days there are excellent views eastward to the Bowland Fells and West Pennine Moors.

❼ Take care and cross the busy A59 alongside the Rufford Arms Hotel and walk down the little lane, Spark Lane, which is directly opposite. At the end of the lane turn right and cross the road bridge over the canal.

❽ On the far side of the bridge cross over and go down the steps to join the towpath of the Rufford branch of the Leeds and Liverpool Canal. Turn left and go under the bridge and follow the towpath for nearly a mile until another road bridge is reached alongside a mooring area. Look out for glimpses of Rufford Old Hall through the trees on the far side of the canal.

❾ Leave the canal at the road bridge and turn right, crossing the bridge and joining the pavement to follow the road back to the village centre. Church Road and St Mary's church are passed on the right. Before the A59 is reached look for Liverpool Road to your left which leads back to the village post office.

PARBOLD

Length: 4 miles

Getting there: The village is situated on the north side of the A5209, roughly halfway between Burscough and Standish. The village centre is reached by turning off the main road at the Stocks Tavern. If approaching from the M6 leave at junction 27.

Parking: There is a small car park alongside the canal in the centre of the village – this is located along Station Road – on the other side of the road bridge to the distinctive wind-mill. If this is full there is ample parking along surrounding village lanes.

Map: OS Landranger 108 Liverpool (GR 491108).

Parbold's status as an affluent dormitory village for executives from Liverpool and Manchester is starkly highlighted by a walk along the main street which uncovers such essential village services as a solicitor's, architects and a sunbed salon. With

good road and rail communications and the natural attraction of the Douglas valley winding its way between hills, it is hardly surprising that Parbold has become a much sought after place to live.

Most of the village's history is linked

FOOD and DRINK

On the junction of the main village street and the A5209 is the Stocks Tavern, a traditional Georgian wayside inn. Telephone: 01257 462902. A wide range of food dishes are available lunchtimes and evenings and include steaks, balti dishes and blackboard specials. The pub is a Tetley's house, but if you prefer Lancashire rather than Yorkshire bitter then try the pretty Greenalls pub next to the old windmill – called the Windmill. Telephone: 01257 462935. A third choice is the Railway Hotel – next to the railway. Telephone: 01257 462917.

with the 18th-century waterway schemes of the Douglas Navigation and the Leeds and Liverpool Canal. The river Douglas was improved by the 1740s giving Wigan coalfields an outlet to the towns of North Lancashire across the Ribble estuary. By 1774 a section of the Leeds and Liverpool Canal was opened from Liverpool to the river Douglas and the complete 127¼ mile canal to Yorkshire was finally opened in 1816. Parbold sprung up at the crossing point of the Douglas and the canal and benefited from the diverse trades which passed by. A further impetus to the village's growth came with the opening of the railway from Wigan to Southport in the 1850s, so beginning Parbold's development as a commuter settlement.

This walk begins at the Leeds and Liverpool Canal in the village centre and follows lanes out of the village before climbing the slopes of Parbold Hill. There are excellent views across the West Lancashire plain and the hill summit is almost reached at the lofty hamlet of High Moor where there is a chance to relax in the comfort of the Rigbye Arms. The walk then goes down the slopes of Parbold Hill and continues across the main road and railway to join the canal in the valley bottom of the river Douglas. From here there is a short towpath walk back to the village centre.

THE WALK

❶ Start at the car park alongside the Leeds and Liverpool Canal with the old windmill on the opposite bank. Leave the car park and turn left to follow Station Road which passes shops and crosses the railway. Continue past more shops then turn immediately right up the adjoining lane – Tan House Lane. Walk the length of the lane and at the top of it cross the adjoining road to the white gates directly opposite.

❷ Go through the white gates and follow the track which runs alongside a primary school. Cross a stile and enter a field and continue along its nearside boundary. Keep to the field edge and when the field begins to slope uphill look out for a footbridge in the tree hedge to your left. Cross the bridge and then veer diagonally right to walk uphill through the next field. Keep on the right-hand side of the large clump of trees in the middle of the field to reach a stile at the next field boundary. Cross this and continue in the same direction uphill. Keep to the left of a small pond surrounded by trees and beyond this a stile next to a gate is reached which leads onto a lane.

❸ Turn right and follow the lane for a very short distance, leaving it on the left-hand side when a stile and footpath sign are reached on your left adjacent to cot-

The Leeds and Liverpool canal.

tages. Follow the nearside boundary down to another stile then continue directly ahead until a wall is reached on your left. Fine views of the Lancashire plain may now be seen looking westwards. Continue along the wall side until a step stile is reached. Cross this to join a track.

❹ Turn right along the track and go through a gateway, then bear right to cross a stile beneath a large quarry warning notice. The path avoids the quarry and runs between a fence and a boundary wall. When this path appears to swing sharp left around the back of the quarry do not miss the stile gap in the fence facing you directly ahead. Cross into this field and walk along the left-hand side of an old hedge line. Ahead of you a stone barn

soon appears and just before reaching it head towards the gate on its left-hand side. To the left of the gate, cross two stiles to join a road.

❺ Turn right and follow the road slightly uphill for about ¼ mile until the hamlet of High Moor is reached by the Rigbye Arms pub. Unless you are stopping for refreshment here continue along High Moor Lane which veers left beyond the phone box. After only 80 yards look out for a footpath sign on the right-hand side of the road at the driveway entrance to Stony Bank House.

❻ Follow this path through the entrance to the property but then quickly leave the driveway on the right by following a

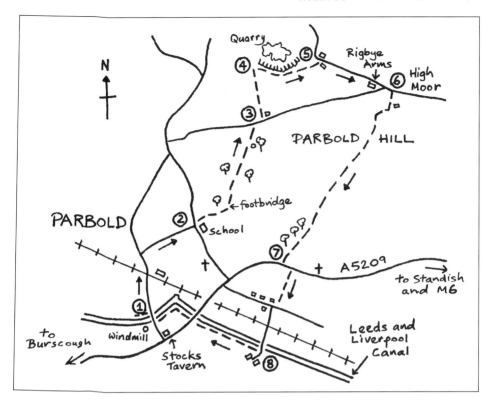

narrow grass path between a high garden hedge and a fence boundary. Go through a gate and the path soon joins a stone track. Turn right and follow this track towards another property, at which point the right of way swings left downhill and runs between tall hedges. Keep to this straight track until it ends rather abruptly facing a field gate. Cross the stile and continue walking downhill in the same straight direction, to reach a gate and stile at the bottom field corner by woodland. The prominent spire of the Sacred Trinity church can be seen ahead, slightly to your left. Cross the stile and continue along the field edge, keeping to the left-hand side of a steep wooded ravine. Walk downhill to reach another stile in the bottom field corner. Cross this and follow the woodland path to emerge alongside the busy A5209 road.

❼ Turn left and follow the roadside pavement uphill for about 130 yards. Then, take care and cross over to the opposite side of the road to join a footpath by the chevron sign where the road starts to bend. Follow this path quite steeply downhill along the nearside fence boundary. The route now descends the lower slopes of Parbold Hill and the Douglas valley can be seen below, carving a way through the hills. At the bottom of the field cross another stile which leads out onto a quiet lane. Turn right and then almost immediately left to continue walking downhill to a level crossing. Cross the railway with care and continue straight ahead until the lane reaches a cobbled canal bridge.

❽   After crossing the bridge turn sharp left to join the canal towpath and left again to walk under the bridge (number 39). Continue in this direction along the towpath for over ½ mile to arrive back in Parbold village. Along the towpath look out for the canal milestone indicating that Leeds is only 99¼ miles away. The towpath then passes under a road bridge and opposite a small basin and the private moorings of newly built houses before climbing up to the main village street alongside the Rocking Horse gift shop. Turn right and cross the bridge over the canal, then left on the opposite side of the road to reach the canalside car park.